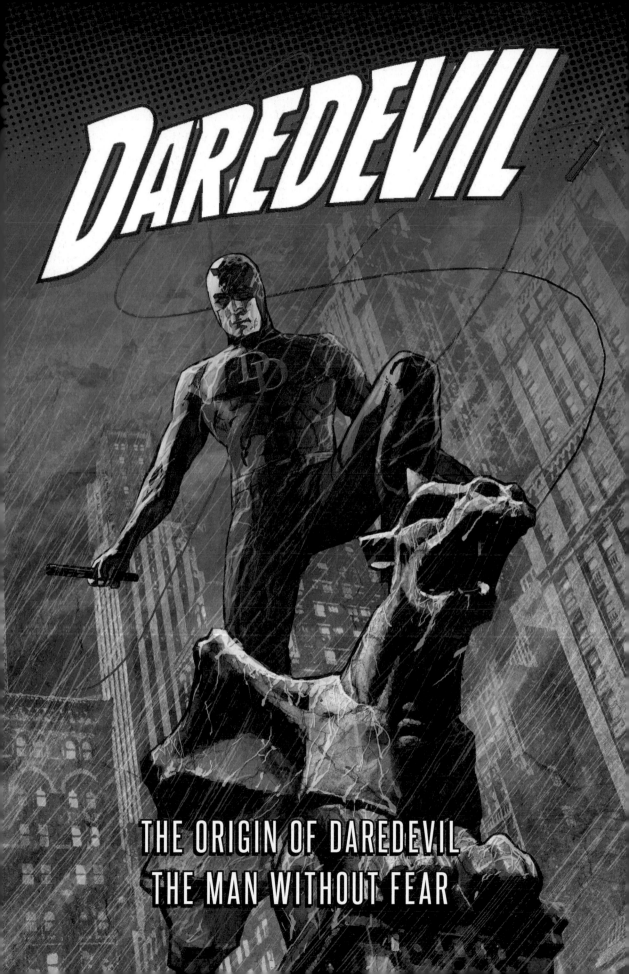

Reader Services

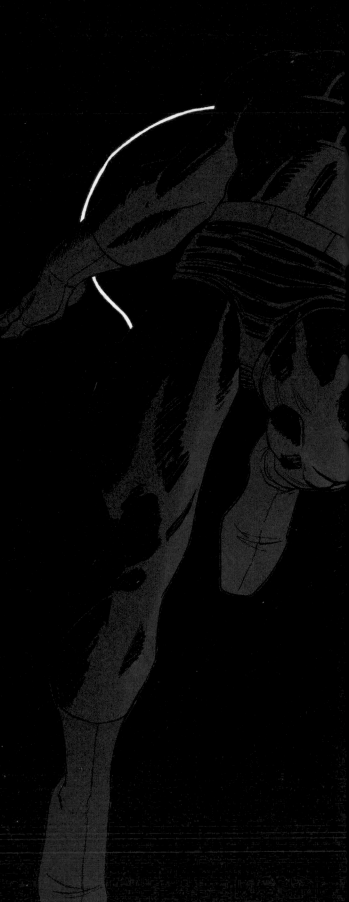

CUSTOMER SERVICE IN THE UK AND REPUBLIC OF IRELAND

How to continue your collection:
Customers can either place an order with their newsagent or receive issues on subscription.
Back issues: Either order through your newsagent or write to: Marvel Collection, Jacklin Enterprises UK, PO Box 77, Jarrow, NE32 3YH, enclosing payment of the cover price plus £1.00 p&p per copy. (Republic of Ireland: cover price plus €1.75).
Subscriptions: You can have your issues sent directly to your home. For details, see insert in issue 1 or phone our Customer Service Hotline on 0333 300 1510 (Monday to Friday, 9am-5pm, calls will be charged at your local rate from a UK landline). Customers from the Republic of Ireland should contact us on 0333 300 1511 (calls will be charged at your local rate from a ROI landline). Alternatively you can write to Marvel's Mightiest Heroes, Jacklin Enterprises UK, PO Box 77, Jarrow, NE32 3YH, or fax your enquiries to 0871 472 4241, or e-mail: mightiestheroes@jacklinservice.com or visit www.mightiestcollection.com

CUSTOMER SERVICE IN OVERSEAS MARKETS

Australia: Back issues can be ordered from your newsagent. Alternatively telephone (03) 9872 4000 or write to: Back Issues Department, Bissett Magazine Services, PO Box 3460, Nunawading Vic 3131. Please enclose payment of the cover price, plus $2.49 inc. GST per issue postage and handling. Back issues are subject to availability.
Subscriptions: You can have your issues sent directly to your home. For details, see insert in issue 1 or phone our Customer Service Hotline on (03) 9872 4000. Alternatively you can write to Hachette subs offer, Bissett Magazine Services, PO Box 3460, Nunawading Vic 3131, or fax your enquiries to (03) 9873 4988, or order online at www.bissettmags.com.au
New Zealand: For back issues, ask your local magazine retailer or write to: Netlink, PO Box 47906, Ponsonby, Auckland.
South Africa: Back issues are available through your local CNA store or other newsagent.
Subscriptions: call (011) 265 4309, fax (011) 314 2984, or write to: Marvel's Mightiest Heroes, Private Bag 10, Centurion 0046 or e-mail: service@jacklin.co.za
Malta: Back issues are only available through your local newsagent.
Malaysia: Call (03) 8023 3260, or e-mail: sales@allscript.com
Singapore: Call (65) 287 7090, or e-mail: sales@allscript.com

Published by Hachette Partworks Ltd, Jordan House, 47 Brunswick Place, London, N1 6EB
www.hachettepartworks.com

Distributed in the UK and Republic of Ireland by Marketforce

This special edition published in 2014 by Hachette Partworks Ltd. forming part of the Marvel's Mightiest Heroes Graphic Novel Collection.

Licensed by Marvel Characters B.V. through Panini S.p.A., Italy. All Rights Reserved.

Printed in Spain.
ISSN: 2051-3992

hachette
PARTWORKS LTD

MARVEL
marvel.com

Contains material originally published in comic form as DAREDEVIL #1 & DAREDEVIL: THE MAN WITHOUT FEAR #1-5. Managing Editor (Hachette Partworks Ltd.), Sarah Gale. Packaged by Panini Publishing, a division of Panini UK Limited. Mike Riddell, Managing Director. Alan O'Keefe, Managing Editor. Ed Hammond, Editor. Samuel Taylor, Editorial Assistant. Marco M. Lupoi, Publishing Director Europe. Will Lucas, Designer. Seb Patrick, Additional Content. Office of publication: Brockbourne House, 77 Mount Ephraim, Tunbridge Wells, Kent TN4 8BS. No similarity between any of the names, characters, persons and/or institutions in this edition with those of any living or dead person or institution is intended, and any such similarity which may exist is purely coincidental. This publication may not be sold, except by authorised dealers, and is sold subject to the condition that it shall not be sold or distributed with any part of its cover or markings removed, nor in a mutilated condition.

DAREDEVIL

SALVADOR LARROCA & CHRIS SOTOMAYOR Cover art

DAREDEVIL #1

STAN LEE Writer & Editor

BILL EVERETT Penciller & Co-Inker

STEVE DITKO & SOL BRODSKY Co-Inkers

SAM ROSEN Letterer

DAREDEVIL: THE MAN WITHOUT FEAR

FRANK MILLER Script

JOHN ROMITA JR. Pencils

AL WILLIAMSON Inks

CHRISTIE SCHEELE Colours

JOE ROSEN Letters

RALPH MACCHIO Series Editor

JOE QUESADA Editor-In-Chief

*I*t's pretty standard for Marvel's heroes to have a certain amount of tragedy in their past. However, when it came to creating Matt Murdock, Stan Lee pretty much threw the book at him! It wasn't bad enough that he was raised in poverty, bullied from an early age and then orphaned as a child – the writer also decided to blind him. (OK, he did boost his other senses to a super-human level but still…) To be honest, it's the sort of history you'd expect for a bitter, revenge-filled super-villain, rather than one of the Marvel Universe's most moral, courageous and honourable super-heroes.

Ed Hammond,
Marvel Editor, Panini UK

We start this volume right at the very beginning with *Daredevil #1*. Written by Stan Lee, with art by Bill Everett, this issue sets up everything you need to know about the blind hero. Sporting his original yellow and red costume (designed by Everett with input from Jack Kirby), this early incarnation is certainly a lot more playful than his modern counterpart. However, the essence of the character is still there. His devotion to stopping criminals, along with a strict set of ethics impressed upon him by his father, create a rigid moral framework within which he operates. To Daredevil, the word of law is sacrosanct and it is his responsibility to make sure no one escapes its hold.

As is to be expected, over the years Daredevil was further tweaked by numerous artists and writers – the most obvious visible change being Wally Wood's redesign of his costume in issue #7. However, there is one creator whose name has become synonymous with the blind hero, producing what many believe to be the defining period for the character – Frank Miller. During his time on the title, new characters, such as the femme fatale Elektra, were introduced, Daredevil's history was further explored, with the addition of hidden clans of ninjas and other mystical oriental figures who sought to control him and, most important of all, the very look of the comic changed. The backdrop of Hell's Kitchen seemed darker and more dangerous than ever before. Much of the action took place on the city's rooftops, turning the Manhattan skyline into a shadowy playground within which heroes and villains fought for their lives. Matt, too, changed. His Catholic upbringing came to the fore, with notions of penance and guilt being regularly alluded to in the comic's subtext. His heroic raison d'être was also brought under intense scrutiny, as the hypocrisy of his chosen role – someone who strives to uphold the law but whose vigilante actions mean he regularly breaks it – came under question.

With this in mind, we absolutely had to pick one of Miller's stories to showcase Daredevil. Beautifully drawn by John Romita Jr, with exceptional inking by the great Al Williamson, 1991's *Man Without Fear* is pretty much the definitive tale of Matt Murdock's rise from bullied child to super-powered lawman.

In a corrupt world he strives to be an incorruptible force, bringing to justice those who defile the rule of law. A mortal who dresses as a demon to do the work of angels, Daredevil is undoubtedly one of the most interesting, morally complex characters the House of Ideas has ever produced.

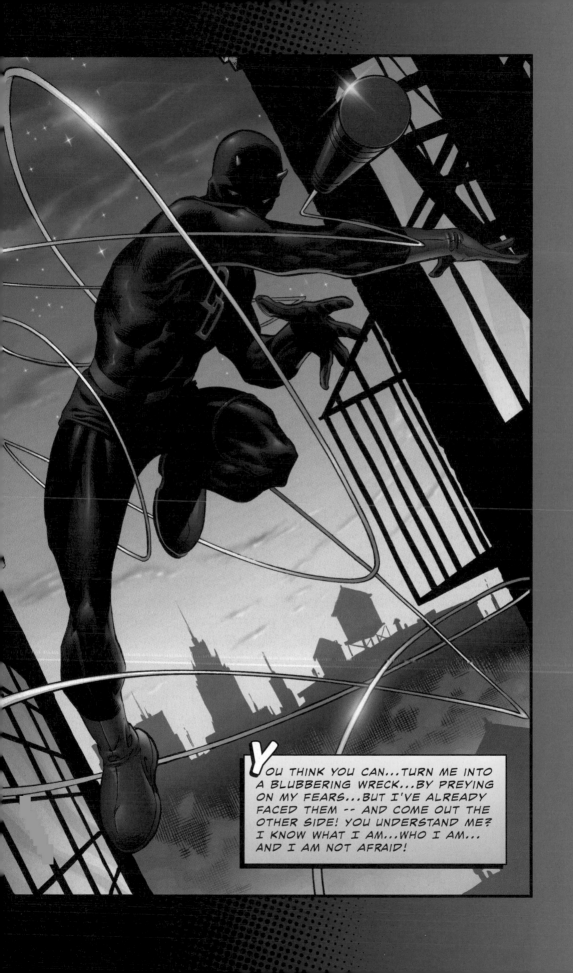

THE ORIGIN OF DAREDEVIL

REMEMBER THIS COVER?

IF YOU ARE ONE OF THE FORTUNATE FEW WHO BOUGHT THIS FIRST COPY-- YOU PROBABLY WOULDN'T PART WITH IT FOR ANYTHING!

NOW WE CONGRATULATE YOU FOR HAVING BOUGHT ANOTHER PRIZED FIRST-EDITION! THIS MAGAZINE IS CERTAIN TO BE ONE OF YOUR MOST VALUED COMIC MAG POSSESSIONS IN THE MONTHS TO COME!

WRITTEN BY....... STAN LEE
ILLUSTRATED BY... BILL EVERETT
LETTERED BY...... SAM ROSEN

YOU ARE LOOKING AT THE ENTRANCE TO FOGWELL'S GYM ON NEW YORK'S LOWER WEST SIDE! IT IS HERE THAT OUR STORY BEGINS... A STORY DIFFERENT FROM ANY YOU HAVE EVER READ BEFORE!

IN A DINGY ROOM ABOVE THE GYM, FOUR MEN PLAY A GAME OF POKER, LITTLE DREAMING OF THE SHOCK WHICH AWAITS THEM!

COME ON, PORKY! WE HAVEN'T GOT ALL DAY! *THE FIXER* MAY BE HERE SOON!

KEEP YOUR SHIRT ON, SAM! I DON'T RUSH FOR *ANYONE!*

WHO DO YOU THINK YOU'RE KIDDIN'? YOU KNOW WHEN THE *FIXER* SNAPS HIS FINGERS, WE *ALL* HOP, IF WE WANNA STAY HEALTHY!

SAM'S RIGHT! ANYHOW, I'M BUSHED! LET'S KNOCK OFF FOR A WHILE UNTIL... HEY! WHAT'S THAT NOISE?

CREAK!

FOR THE LUVVA PETE! WHAT DO YA CALL *THAT?*!!

YOU'RE IN THE WRONG PLACE, BUSTER! WE DON'T USE COSTUMED *WRESTLERS* HERE!

I'VE SEEN NUTTY GETUPS, BUT *THAT* ONE TAKES THE CAKE!

BUT LOOK AT HIS *BUILD!* HANG AROUND, FELLA... MAYBE THE *FIXER* CAN USE YOU!

I INTEND TO DO JUST *THAT!* WHEN I'M THROUGH WITH THE *FIXER*, HE'LL NEVER BE ABLE TO USE ANYONE EVER AGAIN!

HEY, THAT GUY'S HERE LOOKIN' FOR *TROUBLE!* THE FIXER WON'T *LIKE* THAT!!

2

4

OKAY, MISTER... WE'VE *HAD* IT! NOW WHO *ARE* YOU, AND WHAT DO YOU *WANT*?

IT AIN'T *POSSIBLE!* NOBODY CAN FIGHT LIKE THAT! HE MUST DO IT WITH *MIRRORS!!*

NOW THAT PLAY TIME'S OVER, I'LL HANG AROUND UNTIL I FIND THE *FIXER!* AS FOR WHO I *AM*, YOU CAN JUST CALL ME... *DAREDEVIL!!*

"*DAREDEVIL*"! A BRAND NEW NAME IN THE WORLD OF SUPER HEROES! BUT ONE WHICH IS DESTINED TO REACH THE VERY HEIGHTS OF GLORY! FOR *DAREDEVIL* HAS A *SPECIAL* TYPE OF POWER... SUCH AS NO ADVENTURER HAS EVER HAD BEFORE! TO LEARN WHAT IT IS, LET US GO BACK A FEW YEARS... BACK TO THE *ORIGIN* OF THE MAN CALLED

DAREDEVIL!

THE YEAR IS 1950, AS THE PRIZEFIGHTER KNOWN AS *BATTLING MURDOCK* TALKS TO HIS EIGHT-YEAR OLD SON MATTHEW...

BUT I DON'T *WANT* TO STUDY NOW, DAD! WHY CAN'T I GO OUT AND PLAY BALL WITH THE KIDS? I CAN STUDY LATER ON!

NO, MATT! YOU'LL DO IT *NOW!* YOU'LL STUDY EVERY CHANCE YOU GET, HEAR?

I PROMISED YOUR MOTHER, BEFORE SHE DIED, THAT I WOULDN'T LET YOU GROW UP TO BE AN UNEDUCATED PUG LIKE ME! *YOU'RE* GOING TO AMOUNT TO SOMETHING, MATT!

BUT I *WANT* TO BE LIKE YOU, DAD! I'M *PROUD* OF YOU! YOU'RE THE GREATEST...

DON'T SAY IT, BOY! I'M PAST MY PRIME! I'VE NO FUTURE... NOTHING I CAN DO BUT BECOME A PUNCHING BAG FOR YOUNGER MEN!

BUT I WON'T LET THAT HAPPEN TO *YOU!* YOU'RE GONNA *STUDY*... BECOME A LAWYER, OR A DOCTOR ...YOU'LL *BE* SOMEBODY...THE SOMEBODY THAT I CAN NEVER BE!

NOW GO BACK TO YOUR ROOM, SON... AND GET BUSY WITH YOUR *BOOKS!*

OKAY, DAD!

BATTLI MURDO

5

As the years roll by, Matt Murdock does his best to live up to his father's dream!! He becomes top student in his class, forsaking all sports, all athletic activities, although his heart aches for the thrills of the baseball diamond and the gridiron!

IF ONLY DAD WOULD LET ME TRY OUT FOR THE TEAM! I'D BE AS GOOD AS ANY OF THEM... I JUST KNOW I WOULD!

BUT I CAN'T GO AGAINST HIS WISHES! I CAN'T DEFY DAD, AFTER ALL HE'S DONE FOR ME... AFTER ALL HIS SACRIFICES!... I'VE GOT TO BE THE SON HE WANTS ME TO BE!

AND SO, YOUNG MATT MURDOCK GOES HIS LONELY WAY, SPENDING EVERY MINUTE HE CAN SPARE WITH HIS BOOKS, NEVER SHARING IN THE GAMES OF THE OTHER TEEN-AGERS!

THE KIDS ARE INDIAN RASSLING! IF ONLY I COULD GO DOWN AND JOIN THEM!

NO ONE CAN BE AS CRUEL AS AN UNTHINKING YOUTH! IT IS ONLY A MATTER OF TIME BEFORE THE NEIGHBORHOOD KIDS MAKE UP A NICKNAME FOR MATT... A NAME HE WILL LONG REMEMBER...

WELL, WELL! IF IT AIN'T OL' DAREDEVIL HIMSELF!

HI, DAREDEVIL! BE SURE YOU DON'T TIRE YOURSELF OUT TURNING ALL THOSE HEAVY PAGES IN YOUR SCHOOL BOOKS!

THEY'RE LAUGHING AT ME! THEY THINK I'M A SISSY!

THEN, WHEN HE REACHES HIS ROOM...

SOMEDAY I'LL SHOW THEM! I'LL MAKE THEM EAT THOSE WORDS!

I'M AS STRONG AS ANY OF THEM... AS RUGGED AS ANY OF THEM! AND I'LL PROVE IT! SOMEDAY I'LL PROVE IT!!

HIS ANGER BOILING WITHIN HIM, THE RESENTFUL YOUTH STRIKES OUT AT HIS DAD'S PUNCHING BAG, WITH THE PENT-UP FURY OF A THUNDERCLAP...

THE DAY WILL COME WHEN NO ONE WILL EVER LAUGH AT ME AGAIN! WHEN... HEY! I..I KNOCKED THE BAG CLEAN OFF!

6.

THEN, AFTER REPAIRING THE CLASP...

WHAT A *NUMBSKULL* I AM! WHY DON'T I DO THIS *EVERY* DAY!? JUST TO KEEP IN SHAPE!

IT IS ONLY NATURAL THAT THE SON OF BATTLING MURDOCK SHOULD TAKE TO VIGOROUS TRAINING THE WAY A DUCK TAKES TO WATER! AND SO, IN THE MONTHS THAT FOLLOW, WHILE HIS DAD IS OUT OF TOWN ON THE BOXING CIRCUIT...

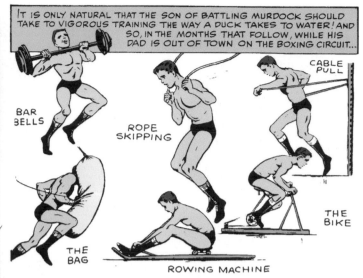

BAR BELLS

ROPE SKIPPING

CABLE PULL

THE BAG

ROWING MACHINE

THE BIKE

BUT, NO MATTER HOW HARD HE TRAINS, THE DETERMINED TEEN-AGER NEVER FORGETS THE GOAL HE HAS SET FOR HIMSELF...

HOW WERE THINGS AT SCHOOL WHILE I WAS AWAY, MATT? EVERY-THING ALL RIGHT, SON?

GUESS SO, DAD... IF YOU CALL STRAIGHT "A'S" ALL RIGHT!

MATT, I KNOW HOW TOUGH IT'S BEEN FOR YOU WHILE THE OTHER KIDS WERE OUT PLAYIN' AND HAVIN' GOOD TIMES! BUT THE DAY WILL COME WHEN YOU'LL *THANK* ME, BOY! YOU'RE GONNA AMOUNT TO SOMETHING... JUST THE WAY YOUR MOTHER WOULD'VE *WANTED* YOU TO!

BUT, THERE IS ONE PROBLEM WHICH BATTLING MURDOCK KEEPS FROM HIS SON...

I HAVEN'T BEEN ABLE TO LAND A FIGHT IN WEEKS! I'M GETTIN' TOO OLD! NO MANAGER WILL TAKE ME! BUT I CAN'T LET MATT DOWN!

I'VE *GOT* TO KEEP FIGHTIN'! UNTIL HE GETS THROUGH COLLEGE! I *OWE* HIM THAT...FOR THE WAY HE'S WORKED ALL THESE YEARS!

FINALLY, IN DESPERATION, MURDOCK MAKES A FATAL DECISION...

LOOK, MURDOCK, YOU'RE ALL WASHED UP, AND YOU KNOW IT! THE ONLY GUY WHO'LL MANAGE A HAS-BEEN LIKE YOU IS THE *FIXER!*

THE *FIXER!* I ALWAYS SWORE TO MYSELF THAT I'D STEER CLEAR OF A GUY WITH *HIS* REPUTATION! BUT NOW I'VE GOT NO CHOICE! I *HAVE* TO GET A FIGHT!

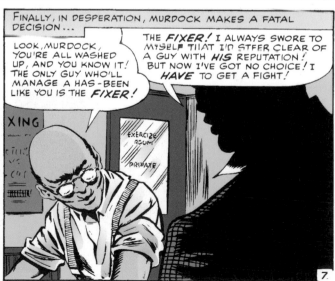

EXERCISE ROOM

PRIVATE

AND SO...

WELL, WELL, IF IT AIN'T BATTLING MURDOCK! TEN YEARS AGO YOU KICKED ME OUT OF YOUR DRESSING ROOM WHEN I OFFERED YOU A DEAL! BUT I KNEW YOU'D COME AROUND, SOONER OR LATER!

SURE, I'LL GET YA SOME FIGHTS! AND YOU WON'T HAVE TO TAKE A DIVE, EITHER! JUST BECAUSE I'M REALLY A SOFT-HEARTED FOOL! HERE, SIGN THIS CONTRACT!

WITH TREMBLING FINGERS, THE MIDDLE-AGED FIGHTER GRASPS THE PEN, AS A DROWNING MAN WOULD CLUTCH AT A STRAW! AND THEN...

THIS IS THE LUCKIEST DAY OF MY LIFE! NOW I'LL BE ABLE TO SEND MATT TO COLLEGE! I DON'T HAVE A THING TO WORRY ABOUT!

EXCITEDLY, THE JOYFUL PRIZE-FIGHTER RUSHES TO HIS APARTMENT, ONLY TO FIND...

MATT! WAIT'LL I TELL YOU THE NEWS! MATT... HE'S NOT HERE!

AS FATE WOULD HAVE IT, MATHEW MURDOCK, AT THAT VERY MOMENT, IS RETURNING FROM THE LIBRARY...TAKING THE MOST IMPORTANT FEW STEPS OF HIS ENTIRE LIFE!

GEE, YOU'D THINK SOMEONE WOULD HELP THAT BLIND MAN ACROSS THE STREET!

SAY, MISTER... CAN I GIVE YOU A HAND?

COZY CLEANERS

HE DIDN'T SEEM TO HEAR ME! HE MIGHT BE DEAF, TOO! SAY...THERE'S A TRUCK TURNING THE CORNER... COMING TOWARDS HIM!

8.

HANK... SLAM ON THE BRAKES! SOMEONE'S CROSSIN' IN FRONT OF US!

I CAN'T! SOMETHING'S WRONG! SHE WON'T STOP!

SCR REECH!

AJAX ATOMIC LABS RADIO-ACTIVE MATERIALS
DANGER

WITHOUT A MOMENT'S HESITATION... HIS SUPPLE MUSCLES RESPONDING TO THE EMERGENCY WITH THE SPEED OF THOUGHT... MATT MURDOCK HURTLES TOWARD THE SCENE OF IMPENDING DISASTER...

HE WON'T HAVE A CHANCE... UNLESS I CAN REACH HIM IN TIME!

THE SWIFT-MOVING TEEN-AGER HURLS THE UNSUSPECTING BLIND MAN OUT OF THE TRUCK'S PATH... BUT HE HIMSELF IS NOT SO FORTUNATE...

OHHH...

HE SAVED THAT MAN'S LIFE!

MOST HEROIC ACT I'VE EVER SEEN!

BUT A CYLINDER FELL FROM THE TRUCK... IT STRUCK HIS FACE! IS... IS IT SOMETHING RADIOACTIVE??

DON'T JUST STAND THERE! SOMEONE CALL AN AMBULANCE!

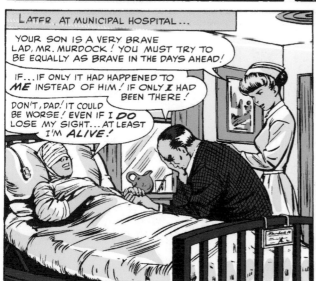

LATER, AT MUNICIPAL HOSPITAL...

YOUR SON IS A VERY BRAVE LAD, MR. MURDOCK! YOU MUST TRY TO BE EQUALLY AS BRAVE IN THE DAYS AHEAD!

IF... IF ONLY IT HAD HAPPENED TO ME INSTEAD OF HIM! IF ONLY I HAD BEEN THERE!

DON'T, DAD! IT COULD BE WORSE! EVEN IF I DO LOSE MY SIGHT... AT LEAST I'M ALIVE!

AND, DAYS LATER, AFTER THE INJURED BOY RETURNS HOME...

GOOD NEWS, MATT! THE DOCTOR'S REPORT SAYS THAT AN OPERATION MAY RESTORE YOUR SIGHT IN A FEW YEARS, AFTER THE TISSUES HAVE HEALED!

THAT'S GREAT, DAD! AND TILL THEN, DON'T WORRY! I'LL STILL KEEP UP MY STUDIES, USING BOOKS WRITTEN IN BRAILLE! I'LL GET MY DIPLOMA YET! YOU'LL SEE!!

9

BUT, IN THE DAYS THAT FOLLOW, MATT MURDOCK STUDIES *MORE* THAN THE WRITTEN WORD! HE BEGINS A STILL MORE INTENSIVE PROGRAM OF PHYSICAL EXERCISES...

I DON'T GET IT! EVER SINCE MY ACCIDENT, I SEEM ABLE TO DO EVERYTHING LOTS BETTER THAN BEFORE... EVEN WITHOUT MY SIGHT!

BONG!!

IT'S AS THOUGH NATURE MADE ALL MY SENSES FAR MORE POWERFUL, TO COMPENSATE FOR MY BLINDNESS!

I WONDER... COULD THE *RADIO-ACTIVE ELEMENTS* WHICH STRUCK MY EYES HAVE ANYTHING TO DO WITH MY INCREASED POWERS?? STRANGER THINGS HAVE BEEN KNOWN TO HAPPEN!

BUT, WHATEVER THE EXPLANATION, IT IS A SUPREMELY CONFIDENT, SELF-ASSURED MATT MURDOCK WHO FINALLY GRADUATES FROM HIGH SCHOOL AND IS EAGERLY ACCEPTED BY THE DIRECTOR OF ADMISSIONS OF STATE COLLEGE, WHERE WE FIND HIM SHARING A DORMITORY ROOM WITH HIS NEW BUDDY, FRANKLIN "FOGGY" NELSON...

D

MATT, YOU OL' HOUND DOG! HOW DO YOU DO IT? I STUDY LIKE A DEMON BUT *YOU* JUST BREEZE THROUGH THE COURSES WITH ALL THE TOP GRADES!

I GUESS MY DAD DESERVES THE CREDIT, FOGGY! HE HAD ME STUDY SO HARD WHEN I WAS YOUNGER, THAT IT ALL SEEMS TO COME EASY TO ME NOW!

AND, I WOULDN'T BE SURPRISED IF THAT RADIATION I ABSORBED IN THE ACCIDENT DOESN'T HAVE SOMETHING TO DO WITH IT, TOO! *EVERYTHING* SEEMS EASY FOR ME NOW! ALL MY SENSES ARE RAZOR SHARP!

"MY *HEARING* IS SO ACUTE, THAT I CAN TELL IF SOMEONE IS IN A ROOM WITH ME JUST BY HEARING THE *HEARTBEAT!*"

"AND I NEVER FORGET AN ODOR ONCE I *SMELL* IT! I COULD RECOGNIZE ANY GIRL BY HER PERFUME... OR ANY MAN BY HIS HAIR TONIC..."

"EVEN MY *FINGERS* HAVE BECOME INCREDIBLY SENSITIVE! I CAN TELL HOW MANY BULLETS ARE IN A GUN JUST BY THE WEIGHT OF THE BARREL."

"WHILE MY SENSE OF *TASTE* HAS BECOME SO HIGHLY DEVELOPED THAT I CAN TELL EXACTLY HOW MANY GRAINS OF SALT ARE ON A PIECE OF PRETZEL..."

10.

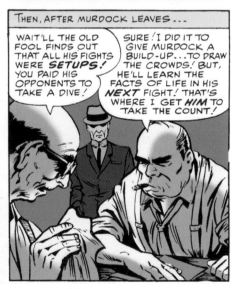

AND SO THE NEXT NIGHT...

THE FIXER SAID I HAVE TO TAKE A DIVE IN THE FIRST ROUND TONIGHT!

...AND IN THIS CORNER, THE MIDDLE-AGED SENSATION... BATTLING MURDOCK!

BUT MY BOY'S HERE TONIGHT, TO ROOT FOR HIS DAD! I'VE ALWAYS TRAINED HIM TO DO HIS BEST... I CAN'T DISAPPOINT HIM NOW!

MURDOCK! YOU FOOL! TAKE IT EASY! WHAT ARE YOU DOIN'?!

IF YOU'RE TRYIN' TO DOUBLE-CROSS ME, YOU'LL LIVE TO REGRET IT! YOU'RE SUPPOSED TO DIVE NOW.. HEAR? DIVE!

HE'S WINNIN', MATT! YOUR DAD'S PULVERIZING HIM!

I KNOW IT! I CAN FOLLOW THE FIGHT PERFECTLY, BY HEARING THE SOUND OF EACH BLOW, EACH FOOTSTEP!

IT'S MY ONE CHANCE! ...MAYBE MY LAST CHANCE... TO DO SOMETHING TO MAKE MY SON PROUD OF ME! I'M NOT GONNA FAIL HIM! I'M GONNA WIN...DO YA HEAR... I'M GONNA WIN!

WHOP!

WHAM!

CALL IT A MIRACLE! CALL IT PURE WILL POWER... SHEER DETERMINATION! CALL IT WHAT YOU WILL, BUT A FEW SECONDS LATER...

THE WINNAH... BATTLING MURDOCK!!

AND THEN, IN THE DRESSING ROOM...

YOU DID IT, DAD! YOU PROVED THAT NOTHING'S IMPOSSIBLE IF A MAN HAS THE COURAGE! IF A MAN'S NOT AFRAID!!

I WANTED YOU TO BE PROUD OF ME, MATT... MY SON!

BUT, IN THE BACK SEAT OF A DARK SEDAN WHICH QUIETLY PULLS AWAY FROM THE STADIUM...

NOBODY DOUBLE-CROSSES THE FIXER! YOU KNOW WHAT TO DO, SLADE!

YEAH, BOSS... I KNOW WHAT TO DO!

12

A FEW MINUTES LATER, AS MATT'S HAPPY FATHER LEAVES THE GYM...

NO MATTER WHAT THE FIXER DOES, I WON'T CARE! MY SON IS *PROUD* OF ME! NOTHING CAN EVER CHANGE THAT NOW!

SUDDENLY, THE SHARP, EXPLOSIVE SOUND OF A GUN SHOT DESTROYS THE SILENCE OF NIGHT, AND ENDS ONE MAN'S REVERIE, FOREVER!

CRACK!

WITHIN SECONDS...

IT'S *BATTLING MURDOCK!* HE WON THE BIG FIGHT TONIGHT!

SOMEBODY MUST HAVE BEEN AWFULLY SORE ABOUT HIS VICTORY! AND WE'RE NOT GOING TO REST UNTIL WE FIND OUT *WHO!!*

NOTHING I CAN DO FOR HIM... IT'S TOO LATE!

LATER, AFTER A GRIEVING MATT MURDOCK HAS HEARD THE TRAGIC NEWS...

YOU'VE GOTTA SNAP OUT OF IT, MATT! PULL YOURSELF TOGETHER, FELLA! THAT'S WHAT YOUR DAD WOULD HAVE WANTED!

WE'LL BE GRADUATING SOON, AND MY DAD'S SETTING ME UP IN A LAW OFFICE! I WANT YOU TO JOIN ME, MATT... AS MY PARTNER!

FINALLY... THE BIG DAY ARRIVES... GRADUATION...

MATTHEW MURDOCK, I AM ESPECIALLY PROUD TO CONGRATULATE YOU FOR BEING CHOSEN CLASS VALEDICTORIAN! YOU HAVE PROVEN THAT AN ALERT MIND AND A STRONG WILL CAN CONQUER ANY OBSTACLES!

THANK YOU, SIR!

AND HE'S GONNA BE MY PARTNER! BOY! CAN I PICK 'EM!

THE NEXT DAY, IN NEW YORK...

WE'RE IN *BUSINESS,* MATT! WITH YOUR BRAINS AND MY DAD'S MONEY, *NOTHING'LL* STOP US!

C'MON IN AND MEET THE SECRETARY I HIRED!

NELSON AND MURDOCK

ATTORNEYS AT LAW

ENTER

MY NAME IS KAREN PAGE, MR. MURDOCK! I HOPE YOU'LL BE PLEASED WITH ME!

HER VOICE IS LIKE MUSIC! FROM THE SOUND, SHE'S FIVE-FEET FOUR, YOUNG, AND I *KNOW* SHE'S LOVELY!

LATER THAT NIGHT, IN THE FURNISHED ROOM MATT HAS RENTED NEAR THE OFFICE...

I'LL *NEVER* BE ABLE TO CONCENTRATE ON MY LAW WORK UNTIL DAD'S MURDERER IS FINALLY BROUGHT TO JUSTICE! BUT YEARS AGO I PROMISED DAD THAT MATT MURDOCK WOULD USE HIS *HEAD*... NEVER BECOME A FIGHTER.. NEVER DEPEND ON MY STRENGTH, THE WAY *DAD* DID!

13.

I CAN'T BREAK THAT PROMISE I MADE! AND YET, WITH MY EXTRA-SHARP SENSES, THERE IS SO *MUCH* I COULD DO! I CAN'T LET ALL MY POWERS GO TO WASTE!

WAIT! I *HAVE* IT!

SNAP!

I'LL SEE TO IT THAT MATT MURDOCK NEVER *DOES* RESORT TO FORCE...BUT SOMEBODY *ELSE* WILL...! SOMEBODY TOTALLY *DIFFERENT* FROM MATT MURDOCK...ALL I NEED ARE SOME OLD SHIRTS WHICH I CAN STITCH TOGETHER!

I'M NO BETSY ROSS, BUT I SHOULD BE ABLE TO HANDLE THIS! LUCKY MY TOUCH IS SO SENSITIVE!

I CAN EVEN BLEND THE *COLORS*, FOR EACH COLORED FABRIC HAS A DIFFERENT *FEEL* TO ME!

A FEW HOURS LATER...

THERE! WHENEVER I DON THIS COSTUME, I'LL NO LONGER *BE* MATT MURDOCK! BUT I'LL NEED A *NEW* NAME! WHAT IF THE KIDS IN THE OLD NEIGHBORHOOD COULD SEE ME NOW!! THE KIDS WHO TAUNTED ME...CALLED ME "DAREDEVIL"! *WAIT!* THAT'S IT!!

"DAREDEVIL" THEY CALLED ME... BUT THEY MEANT IT AS AN INSULT! WELL, THAT'S WHO I'LL *BE*... THE NAME IS *PERFECT!*

THE COSTUME IS TIGHT ENOUGH TO WEAR UNDER MY CLOTHES IF NEED BE! I'LL JUST MAKE A FEW FINISHING TOUCHES ON THE HEADPIECE! WHEN I'M THROUGH, *DAREDEVIL* WILL BE RECOGNIZED *ANYWHERE!!*

EVEN THOUGH I DON'T *NEED* IT, I'LL CONTINUE TO CARRY A CANE AS MATT MURDOCK! MMM...THAT GIVES ME ANOTHER IDEA! THAT CANE WOULD MAKE A GREAT WEAPON FOR *DAREDEVIL!*

THROUGH THE LONG NIGHT, THE UNSEEING MAN WORKS ...HIS SUPER-SENSITIVE FINGERS MOLDING AND MANIPULATING HIS CANE FAR MORE PRECISELY THAN ANY NORMAL CRAFTSMAN MIGHT DO IT!

FLEXIBLE HANDLE

I'LL HINGE IT IN THE MIDDLE... DESIGN A SHEATH FOR IT...IT'LL BE THE PERFECT ALL-PURPOSE WEAPON!

HINGE

14

IT'S *PERFECT!*

I CAN USE IT IN A HUNDRED WAYS!

BONG!

AND NOW FOR THE JOB AT HAND! I'VE GOT TO BRING MY FATHER'S MURDERER TO JUSTICE! TOMORROW'S SATURDAY! THE OFFICE WILL BE CLOSED...SO I'LL START IN THE MORNING!

AND I KNOW JUST WHERE TO BEGIN!

AND SO:.. DAD'S MANAGER WAS A MAN CALLED THE *FIXER!* I HAVE A HUNCH HE *DESERVES* THAT NICKNAME!

HOW *CON-FIDENTLY* THAT BLIND YOUNG MAN WALKS THROUGH THE STREET!

UNERRINGLY GUIDED BY HIS ATOM-INDUCED RADAR-SENSE, MATT MURDOCK REACHES HIS DESTINATION...

THIS WILL BE *DAREDEVIL'S* FIRST TEST! NOW TO CHANGE CLOTHES IN AN ALLEY AND SEE IF I'M AS GOOD AS I THINK!

AND SO WE RETURN TO THE PRESENT, AS OUR DAREDEVIL SAGA CONTINUES...

NOW, DO YOU TAKE ME TO THE *FIXER,* OR...?

OR, *NOTHING!* WE'VE *HAD* IT, FELLA! JUST HANG AROUND...HE'LL BE HERE ANY MINUTE!

SOMEBODY *ASKIN'* FOR ME? WHAT DO YA WANT?

HEY, BOSS, DIG THE GETUP ON THAT CLOWN!

HE LOOKS LIKE *TROUBLE* TO ME, FIXER! WANT WE SHOULD LEAN ON 'IM A LITTLE?

MY "ASSOCIATES" DON'T SEEM TO LIKE YOUR LOOKS, MISTER! YOU BETTER TALK FAST!

FROM THE HEAVY TONE OF HIS VOICE HE'S BEEFY, ROUGH! I HEAR BREATHING ON EACH SIDE OF HIM... SO THE OTHER TWO MUST BE FLANKING HIM!

CORRECTION, FIXER! *YOU'RE* THE ONE WHO'S GOING TO TALK!!

15.

NOW LET'S ALL SETTLE DOWN FOR A NICE TALK... UNLESS YOU'D LIKE ANOTHER SESSION WITH ME!

LOOK, YOU...

QUIET! I'LL HANDLE THIS! I'M STILL THE BOSS!

SLAM!

MISTER, WHOEVER YOU ARE...YOU'RE IN A MESS OF TROUBLE! YOU'RE NOT GETTIN' AWAY WITH COMIN' HERE AND ROUGHING US UP! WE GOT LAWS TO PROTECT INNOCENT PEOPLE! SAM, CALL THE COPS!!

THE SOUND OF A HAND PICKING UP A RECEIVER! THIS IS ALMOST TOO EASY!

YEOWP!

CLANK!

FIXER, I SUSPECT YOU WERE RESPONSIBLE FOR THE DEATH OF BATTLING MURDOCK! WHY DON'T YOU CONFESS NOW AND SAVE US ALL A LOT OF TROUBLE!?

YOU'RE NUTS! I HAD NOTHIN' TO DO WITH IT! I GOT A PERFECT ALIBI!

I HAVE ANOTHER POWER I WASN'T EVEN AWAKE UP! I CAN HEAR HIS PULSE RATE! IT'S SPEEDING UP, INDICATING HE'S LYING! MY SUPER-SENSE OF HEARING IS LIKE A BUILT-IN LIE DETECTOR!

MAYBE YOU DO HAVE AN ALIBI! MAYBE YOURS WASN'T THE FINGER THAT SQUEEZED THE TRIGGER! BUT YOU GAVE THE ORDER... DIDN'T YOU??

NO! NO! STAY BACK!! STOP HIM, YOU GUYS...DON'T LET 'IM GET ME!

17.

HE KNOWS TOO MUCH!! HE MIGHT EVEN KNOW *I'M* THE MURDERER! CAN'T TAKE ANY CHANCES!

SO INTENT IS DAREDEVIL UPON LISTENING TO THE FIXER'S PULSE RATE, TO DETERMINE IF HE IS THE GUILTY MAN, THAT HIS ULTRA-SHARP HEARING SENSE REACTS A FRACTION OF A SECOND TOO SLOW, AND...

IT WAS *ME*... BUT YOU'LL NEVER BE ABLE TO *DO* ANYTHING ABOUT IT!

BEHIND ME!! SOMEONE... OHHH!

A NORMAL MAN, WITH ALL HIS SENSES, MIGHT BE DOOMED IN SUCH A SITUATION! BUT, THE MOMENT THE FEARLESS *DAREDEVIL* FEELS HIMSELF HURTLING INTO SPACE, HIS SUPER-KEEN EARS CATCH THE RUSTLING OF A FLAG, AS HIS LIGHTNING-FAST REFLEXES GO INTO ACTION...

A FLAGPOLE ALONGSIDE ME... ONLY ONE CHANCE!!

PRESSING THE HIDDEN STUD WHICH RELEASES HIS CANE HANDLE AT THE SAME SPLIT SECOND AS HE LUNGES OUT, HE STOPS HIS FALL IN MIDAIR!!

GOT IT!!

FROM HERE ON IN, IT'S ALL A BREEZE!

NOW THEN, GENTS... WHERE *WERE* WE??

HE'S BACK!!

WHUMP!

MEANWHILE, AT THE OTHER SIDE OF TOWN...

FUNNY, MATT DOESN'T ANSWER! MAYBE HE'S STILL ASLEEP! OH...THE DOOR'S OPEN!

HEY, LAZYBONES! I THOUGHT I'D SEE IF YOU *NEED* ANYTHING, AND...MATT?? HE'S *GONE!*

GOSH, I WISH HE'D *CALLED* ME! I HATE TO THINK OF POOR MATT WALKING AROUND TOWN ALL ALONE, WITH ALL THE TRAFFIC IN NEW YORK!

18.

I'LL GO UP TO THE OFFICE...MAYBE HE DECIDED TO COME HERE AND GET FAMILIAR WITH THE PLACE BEFORE STARTING WORK ON MONDAY!

BUT, ENTERING THE NEW OFFICE, FOGGY FINDS IT UNOCCUPIED, EXCEPT FOR THE MOST DECORATIVE ACCESSORY...

KAREN! TODAY'S YOUR DAY OFF!

I KNOW, MR. NELSON! BUT I'M A STRANGER IN NEW YORK, AND HAD NO ONE TO VISIT, SO I THOUGHT I'D TIDY UP THE OFFICE WHILE I HAD A CHANCE! IS MR. MURDOCK WITH YOU?

NO! MATTER OF FACT, I HOPED HE'D BE HERE! I DON'T LIKE HIM WANDERING AROUND TOWN ALONE!

I UNDERSTAND! WHAT A PITY SUCH A WONDERFUL, HANDSOME MAN IS SO HANDICAPPED!

WOW! I'D SURE LIKE TO HEAR HER TALK ABOUT ME IN THAT ADORING TONE OF VOICE!

DON'T LET HIS BLINDNESS FOOL YOU, KAREN! HE'S STILL THE SMARTEST, MOST CAPABLE, MOST COURAGEOUS FELLA I KNOW! HE DOESN'T EVEN SEEM TO MIND NOT SEEING!

THERE'S SOMETHING ABOUT HIM THAT MAKES A GIRL WANT TO TAKE HIM IN HER ARMS AND... OH, I'M SORRY, MR. NELSON! I HAD NO RIGHT TO SPEAK THAT WAY! IT'S JUST THAT HE SEEMS TO NEED SOMEONE TO LOOK AFTER HIM!

IT WOULD BE HARD TO IMAGINE KAREN PAGE'S FEELINGS IF SHE COULD SEE THE "HANDICAPPED" MAN SHE IS REFERRING TO AT THIS MOMENT...

OUT, ALL OF YOU! I'M ONLY INTERESTED IN SLADE AND THE FIXER!

BOY...YOU DON'T HAVETA TELL ME TWICE!

COME BACK, YOU ROTTEN COWARDS! DON'T LEAVE US WITH 'IM!

NOW, YOU TWO, I'VE LEARNED WHAT I WANTED! SLADE ACTUALLY DID THE SHOOTING, BUT YOU GAVE THE ORDER!

WHAT GOOD'LL IT DO YOU?? YOU CAN'T PROVE IT!

YEAH! WHERE'S YOUR EVIDENCE??

19.

NOW FOR MY FINAL BLUFF! THEY'RE SO WORRIED NOW, THEY'LL BELIEVE *ANYTHING!*

RIGHT *HERE!* I HAVE A MINIATURE TAPE RECORDER CONCEALED IN MY BILLY CLUB! IT'LL TELL THE POLICE ALL THEY NEED TO KNOW!

HE'S *GOT* US!

THEN, BEFORE DAREDEVIL CAN MAKE A MOVE, THE FIXER TRIES ONE LAST, DESPERATE MANEUVER...

QUICK, SLADE... *RUN!* BEFORE HE CAN GET HIS BALANCE!

OHHH...

MY ARM! I WRENCHED IT! I WAS A FOOL FOR BEING SO OVERCONFIDENT! I SHOULD HAVE *KNOWN* THEY'D MAKE ONE FINAL TRY TO ESCAPE!

THEY CAN'T HAVE GOTTEN FAR! I'LL GET THEM *YET!*

BUT, RACING AROUND THE CORNER, SLADE AND THE FIXER QUICKLY MINGLE WITH THE SATURDAY AFTERNOON SHOPPING CROWD...

HE'LL NEVER FIND US NOW, IN THE MIDDLE OF THIS CROWD!

JUST THE SAME, KEEP MOVING! THERE'S NO TELLIN' *WHAT* THAT GUY CAN DO!

MEANWHILE...

I CAN STILL SMELL THE TRACES OF THE FIXER'S CIGAR SMOKE! I CAN FOLLOW THE SCENT LIKE A BLOODHOUND... BUT I'LL BE ABLE TO GET AROUND EASIER IN THE CROWD *WITHOUT* A COSTUME!!

AND SO BEGINS ONE OF THE STRANGEST PURSUITS ON RECORD, AS A MAN WITHOUT SIGHT UNERRINGLY MAKES HIS WAY THROUGH A CROWDED AVENUE, ON THE TRAIL OF TWO KILLERS!

I'M GLAD HIS CIGAR IS A STRONG ONE! HE MIGHT AS WELL BE *TELLING* ME WHERE HE IS... BUT HE DOESN'T *KNOW* IT!!

20.

WITHIN MINUTES, THE GRACEFUL, SUPPLE FIGURE OF MATT MURDOCK HAS KNIFED THROUGH THE UNSUSPECTING CROWD LIKE A SHADOWY WRAITH, AND THEN...

I HOPE THEY'RE STAYING TOGETHER! I WANT TO BRING THEM *BOTH* TO JUSTICE! THE CIGAR SCENT IS STRONGER NOW...I'M ALMOST UP TO THEM!

SLOW DOWN, SLADE! WE'RE SAFE NOW! HE'S NOWHERE IN SIGHT!

GUESS YOU'RE RIGHT! NO ONE NEAR US NOW BUT THAT BLIND GUY! WE'VE LOST 'IM FOR SURE!

C'MON, WE'LL DUCK INTO THAT SUBWAY STATION ACROSS THE STREET AND GET OFF AT PENN STATION! WE'LL BE OUTTA TOWN IN AN HOUR!

THAT'S WHAT *THEY* THINK!

HEY! DIDJA SEE HOW FAST THAT BLIND GUY PUSHED PAST US?

WHO CARES? WE GOT OUR *OWN* PROBLEMS!

BUT UNKNOWN TO THE FLEEING DUO, THEIR PROBLEMS ARE JUST *BEGINNING!* FOR, DIRECTLY *AHEAD* OF THEM...

THEIR FOOTSTEPS ARE GETTING CLOSER! I'LL JUST MAKE IT!!

GOING SOMEWHERE, BOYS?!

IT'S HIM!!

IT...IT AIN'T *POSSIBLE!*

SEPARATE! HE CAN'T GET US *BOTH!!!!*

I WAS *AFRAID* THEY'D TRY THAT!

I CAN TELL BY THE UNBROKEN SOUND OF SLADE'S FOOTSTEPS, THERE'S NO ONE BETWEEN US! ...SO IT'S SAFE TO THROW MY CANE!

GOOD! HE'S TACKLING *SLADE!* THAT MEANS *I'LL* ESCAPE!

21.

DON'T YOU KNOW ENOUGH TO STAY WHERE I LEFT YOU??

UHH!!

NOW FOR MY LAST BLUFF!

THE FIXER JUST TOLD US EVERYTHING, SLADE! HE'S INNOCENT! YOU ARE MURDOCK'S MURDERER!

THE DIRTY CRUMB! HE'S NOT GONNA WIGGLE OUT OF THIS! HE'S AS GUILTY AS I AM! I ONLY PULLED THE TRIGGER.. BUT HE GAVE THE ORDERS!

HEAR ENOUGH, BOYS??

WE SURE DID!

BUT...

WAIT! WHO ARE YOU?

THE NAME'S DAREDEVIL... REMEMBER IT! YOU'LL BE HEARING IT AGAIN... I PROMISE!!

NOT LONG AFTERWARDS...

MATT! SAY, I WAS WORRIED ABOUT YOU, FELLA! WHERE'VE YOU BEEN?

JUST OUT FOR A WALK, FOGGY! I'D HAVE BEEN HERE SOONER, BUT AS YOU KNOW.. I CAN'T GET AROUND TOO FAST!

WE JUST HAD A CALL, MR. MURDOCK! AN ACCUSED MURDERER, NAMED SLADE... HE WANTED TO KNOW IF WE'D DEFEND HIM!

BUT I TURNED HIM DOWN! FROM THE POLICE REPORT, I WAS CONVINCED HE'S GUILTY! HOPE YOU DON'T MIND, MATT!

MIND??

NO! I DON'T MIND AT ALL! NOT A BIT! NOT ONE SINGLE BIT!

DAD, WHEREVER YOU ARE...I KINDA HOPE YOU'RE RESTING EASIER NOW!

DON'T WASTE A MINUTE!! WE CAN'T WAIT TO HEAR WHAT YOU THINK OF DAREDEVIL!! SEND YOUR LETTERS TO DAREDEVIL, c/o STAN LEE, 3RD FLOOR, 655 MADISON AVE, N.Y.C. 21 AND IN THE MEANTIME, REMEMBER.. THIS IS JUST THE BEGINNING! WE'VE ONLY SCRATCHED THE SURFACE.!! DAREDEVIL REALLY HITS HIS STRIDE IN ISH #2, WHEN HE FACES HIS FIRST SUPER-VILLAIN! DON'T MISS IT!!

D

23.

BUT YOU HAVE TO BE *SNEAKY* IF YOU DON'T WANT TO GET *YELLED* AT.

MATT IS *VERY, VERY* SNEAKY.

THE NEXT MORNING.

OFFICER LIEBOWITZ IS DOING WHAT HE *ALWAYS* DOES.

HE'S TAKING ALL THE *FUN* OUT OF *EVERYTHING.*

YOU WAS *BREAKING* THE *LAW.* THAT THERE *FIRE HYDRANT* IS *CITY PROPERTY* AND YOU WAS *PLAYING* IN IT.

WE WASN'T *HURTING* NOBODY!

FSHHH

YOU'RE JUST AN OLD *BLOWHEAD!*

YOU WATCH HOW YOU ADDRESS A *POLICE OFFICER,* YOUNG LADY--

-- OR I'LL ROUND THE PACK OF YOU *UP.*

WHY CAN'T YOU ALL LEARN TO *BEHAVE*--

--LIKE THE *MURDOCK* BOY? HE'S *NEVER* IN TROUBLE, IS HE?

HEY!

COME BACK HERE!

GO! GO! GO!

THAT THERE CLUB IS CITY PROPERTY!

HUFF HUFF HUFF WHO WAS THAT KID?...

THE BOY'S HEART FEELS LIKE IT'S GOING TO EXPLODE.

IT'S A GREAT FEELING.

BUT DAD WOULD BE REALLY SORE IF HE KNEW WHAT MATT'S DONE.

SO MATT TAKES THE NIGHTSTICK TO HIS FAVORITE PLACE.

A PLACE THAT SMELLS OF SAWDUST AND OLD SWEAT.

THE GYM.

...BATTLIN' JACK MURDOCK.

MATT'S DAD.

HE WAS THE BEST, IN HIS DAY.

MATT HEADS HOME AND HOPES DAD WON'T BE SAD AGAIN TONIGHT.

BUT THERE HE IS WITH THAT OLD PHOTOGRAPH AGAIN.

HE NEVER SAYS WHO SHE WAS...

MAGGIE...

...I'M SORRY, MAGGIE... I'M...

COME ON, DAD. LET'S GET YOU ON TO BED.

HNH?

...RIGHT, SON, YOU'RE A GOOD BOY, MATT.

A GOOD BOY, GOD BLESS YOU...

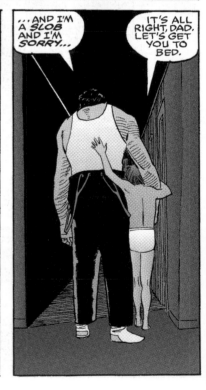

...AND I'M A SLOB AND I'M SORRY...

IT'S ALL RIGHT, DAD, LET'S GET YOU TO BED.

THE GYM.

A DIFFERENT KIND OF ROUGH NIGHT FOR *JACK MURDOCK*.

WHUDD WHUDD WHUDD

WISE UP, MURDOCK. SLADE DOESN'T GET *TIRED* REAL EASY--

--AND I'M AFRAID HE'S STARTING TO *ENJOY* HIMSELF.

KHAFF

LET HIM...

THE *FIXER'S* TRYING TO DO YOU A *FAVOR*, YOU *DORK*.

A REGULAR *JOB* AIN'T SO EASY TO *COME BY*, THESE DAYS.

I WON'T...

YOU *WILL*.

YOU'LL WORK THE *NEIGHBORHOOD* FOR ME--COLLECT ON BAD *DEBTS*--OR YOU WILL *DIE*.

SO KILL ME. I WON'T WORK FOR THE MOB.

I WASN'T *FINISHED*, MURDOCK. YOU WILL *COLLECT* UNPAID *PROTECTION MONEY*--OR YOU WILL *DIE*--

--AND SO WILL YOUR BRIGHT-EYED *BOY*. YOUR LITTLE *MATT*.

THERE ARE TIMES WHEN JACK MURDOCK DOES NOT HATE HIMSELF.

ONLY IN THE RING, ONLY IN THE HEAT OF COMBAT, WHEN HIS FISTS ARE SURE AND HIS LEGS ARE STRONG--

--AND HE FEELS HIMSELF AGAIN...

...AND HE FOR-GETS THE WAY HE SPENDS HIS DAYS...

...ONLY IN THE HEAT OF IT--

--WHEN HE IS A WARRIOR--

-- NOT A MOB ENFORCER.

WHEN HE IS A CHAMPION--

--NOT A THUG.

BUT IT KEEPS *FOOD* ON THE TABLE. IT KEEPS *MATT* FED. IT BUYS MATT'S *SHOES.*

AND ALL IT *COSTS JACK MURDOCK* IS HIS SOUL.

MORALES COULD ONLY PAY UP *HALF,* FIXER.

THAT'S *MISTER* FIXER TO YOU, MURDOCK.

AND *HALF* AIN'T *ALL* OF IT, IS IT? *TALK* TO HIM AGAIN. HARDER.

HOME, AND MATT.

YOU *PROMISE* ME, SON,

BUT I CAN'T STUDY *ALL* THE TIME, DAD.

AND THE *GUYS--* THEY CALL ME A *SISSY.* IT MAKES ME REALLY *MAD.*

IT MAKES ME WANT TO *SOCK* THEM AND I DON'T SEE ANY REASON WHY I *SHOULDN'T.*

YOU'D HAVE SOCKED THEM. *YOU'D* HAVE SOCKED THEM *GOOD.*

YEAH. I WOULD'VE.

AND LOOK WHERE MY FISTS HAVE GOTTEN ME.

WE OWE IT TO YOUR *MOTHER,* MATT. YOU'VE GOT TO BE SOMETHING *SPECIAL.* YOU'VE GOT TO BE *NOTHING* LIKE *ME.*

YOU *PROMISE* ME, SON.

MATT *PROMISES--*

--BUT, A FEW WEEKS LATER, ON THE KIND OF DAY WHEN THE NEW YORK *HEAT* BRINGS RAISED *VOICES* AND CLENCHED *FISTS...*

...MATT MURDOCK PROVES HIMSELF TO BE HIS FATHER'S SON.

DAD! I FINALLY *SHOWED* THAT *BARKLEY* KID!

HE TOOK A *POKE* AT ME AND I POKED HIM *RIGHT BACK!*

HE JUST *SAT DOWN* AND LOOKED *DUMB!* IT WAS *GREAT!*

DAMN IT, MATT.

DAMN IT!

KUFF

THEN DAD IS ALL *TEARS* AND *REGRET* AND MATT IS RUNNING FROM THEIR HOME, THROUGH THE CITY, DIRECTIONLESS, LOST.

HE HIT ME. THE THOUGHT IS SO *BIG*, SO *CRAZY*.

DAD *HIT* ME.

IT WAS WRONG.

DAD WAS WRONG.

AND IF EVEN DAD CAN BE WRONG, THEN *ANYBODY* CAN DO BAD THINGS. ANYBODY AT ALL.

THE ONLY WAY TO *STOP* PEOPLE FROM BEING BAD IS TO MAKE *RULES*. LAWS.

SOMEWHERE IN A LONG AND LONELY NIGHT THE BOY'S COURSE IS SET.

HE WILL STUDY THE *RULES*.

HE WILL STUDY THE *LAWS*.

IT IS A *COSTLY* CHOICE.

EVERY *NIGHT*-- EVERY *WEEKEND*-- MATT HAS TO *FIGHT* THE URGE TO LEAVE HIS LITTLE ROOM--

--AND ANSWER THE ENDLESS *TAUNTS* OF OTHER KIDS.

THE *WORST* OF IT IS THE *NICKNAME* THEY GIVE HIM.

HEY, DAREDEVIL! COME ON *OUT!*

DAREDEVIL!

RECESS BECOMES *PURGATORY.*

BUT MATT DOES NOT *FIGHT.*

HE OBEYS THE RULES.

AND STILL THEY CHANT...

DAREDEVIL

DAREDEVIL

DAREDEVIL

YOU COULD'VE FOUGHT *BACK,* MATT, YOU'RE SUCH A *WEENIE.*

HIS FAVORITE PLACE.

THE GYM.

ENDLESS STOLEN HOURS.

HIS SECRET TIME--

AT THE BAG.

--WHEN HIS *FISTS* ARE LIKE *MACHINE GUN FIRE*--DROWN- ING OUT HIS ANGRY SOBS...

...AND, UNNOTICED BY MATT, SOMEONE OBSERVES, AND WAITS...

A SHADOW, UNMOVING, SILENT, FEELING THE BOY'S FURY...

...AND WAITING FOR THE DAY THE BOY WILL MEET HIS DESTINY.

IT'S A PICTURE PERFECT DAY. ONE MATT WILL NEVER FORGET.

THE LAST HE WILL EVER SEE.

A HELPLESS OLD BLIND MAN-- A CAREENING TRUCK--

--A DECISION MADE FASTER THAN THOUGHT--

--GALLONS OF HORRID, SPEWING MUCK--

--PAIN--

--AND DARKNESS--

--BRAVEST THING I EVER SAW! BUT HIS FACE-- HIS EYES...

MY GOD-- THAT STUFF IN HIS EYES-- --IS IT RADIOACTIVE?

YES...

...YES, IT COURSES THROUGH HIS BLOOD. IT CHANGES HIM.

HIS BLOOD. IT BURNS...

...IT GUSHES THROUGH HIGH POWER HOSES AND SLAMS AGAINST THE BASE OF HIS SKULL.

EVERYTHING HURTS.

HE DOESN'T KNOW WHERE HE IS.

SANDPAPER SCRAPES HIS SKIN EVERY TIME HE MOVES--NO--NOT SANDPAPER--SHEETS-- STARCHED SHEETS--

--AND THE SMELLS... CHEMICAL SMELLS. DISINFECTANTS.

HOSPITAL, HE THINKS. I'M IN A HOSPITAL.

PEOPLE COME AND GO, SMELLING LIKE BATHTUBS FULL OF SWEAT--LIKE EATEN FOOD--LIKE ITALIAN SAUCES AND HALF- DIGESTED EGGS--

--THEY STAB HIM WITH NEEDLES AND FILL HIM FULL OF DRUGS BUT DRUGS DON'T FOOL HIM. HE KNOWS THEY CUT HIS FACE.

EVERYTHING HURTS.

ALL HE WANTS IS TO DIE.

BUT HE *DOESN'T DIE.* SO HE HAS TO *MAKE DO.*

AFTER A WHILE HE SOMEHOW *SHUTS IT OUT.*

WHAT'S HAPPENED TO HIM?

WHAT HAS HE BECOME?

DAD DOESN'T UNDERSTAND. NOBODY UNDERSTANDS.

EXCEPT THE *WOMAN.* THE STRANGER WHO COMES.

SHE *SOOTHES* HIM. SHE CALLS THESE CRAZY *SENSES* A *BLESSING* AND MAKES HIM PROMISE TO KEEP THEM A *SECRET.* EVEN FROM *DAD.*

SHE KISSES HIS *FOREHEAD.* HER LIPS ARE *SOFT* AND *LOVING...*

...AND SOMETHING HARD DANGLES FROM HER NECK...

...IT'S A CROSS. MADE OF GOLD.

SHE LEAVES, TAKING HER MYSTERY WITH HER.

BUT HE FEELS *CALMER* NOW. *STRONGER.*

HE WILL *SURVIVE THIS.*

HE WILL *SURVIVE THIS.*

--IF YOU TALK TO THE *PRESS* OR MAKE ANY ATTEMPT TO FILE A *COMPLAINT* AGAINST US--

--WE'LL REVEAL YOUR *OWN* INVOLVEMENT WITH THE *FIXER.*

YOUR BOY IS *BLIND.* NOTHING CAN *CHANGE* THAT. DO YOU WANT HIM TO BE THE SON OF A *CONVICT,* AS WELL?

WEEKS GO BY.

EVERYBODY *PITIES* MATT.

EVERYBODY WANTS TO HELP HIM CROSS THE *STREET.*

BUT THERE IS NO PITY IN THE MAN WHO TRAILS HIM.

NO PITY. NO MERCY.

ONLY COLD CLEAR *PURPOSE.*

AND NOW THE TIME HAS COME TO SEE WHAT MATT MURDOCK IS *MADE OF.*

THAT NIGHT. IN THE GYM.

IT USED TO BE MATT'S FAVORITE PLACE--

--BUT NOW IT'S FILLED WITH CRIES OF FRUS-TRATION--TEARFUL FURY--

--AND LOW SOBS THAT SPEAK OF DEFEAT.

HE CAN'T SEE.

HE CAN'T SEE.

HE'S USELESS.

QUIT FEELING SORRY FOR YOURSELF. GET UP.

WHO?...

HE CALLS HIMSELF STICK...

...AND ONCE HE STARTS TALKING, HE DOESN'T STOP.

HE TAKES MATT TO A DIRTY, DUSTY BASEMENT.

I WAS *BORN BLIND, KID.* ON THE *STREET.* AND I MADE MY *WAY.* SO DON'T GIVE WITH ANY MORE *BELLY-ACHING* OR I'LL *FLATTEN* YOU.

YOU'LL TRAIN *HERE.* EVERY SPARE HOUR YOU *HAVE.* IF YOU'RE *GOOD* ENOUGH, I'LL MAKE YOU A *WARRIOR.*

I'M NOT SAYING YOUR CHANCES ARE *GOOD.* YOU'RE *UN-DISCIPLINED. IN-DULGENT. EMOTION-AL.* BUT I'M TAKING A *CHANCE* WITH YOU-- BECAUSE I NEED ALL THE HELP I CAN *GET.*

WHAT KIND OF HELP?

NO QUESTIONS. HOLD OUT YOUR HAND. CON-CENTRATE.

FEEL THE *AIR.*

BUT THERE'S NO *WIND.*

SHUT UP. CONCENTRATE.

THE AIR'S *FILLING* THE ROOM. ONE WALL'S *CLOSER* THAN THE OTHER. *FEEL* IT.

NOW THE *OTHER* WALL. FEEL IT.

CONCENTRATE.

CONCENTRATE.

BUT THERE'S NOTHING *THERE!*

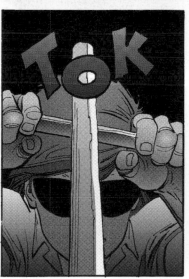

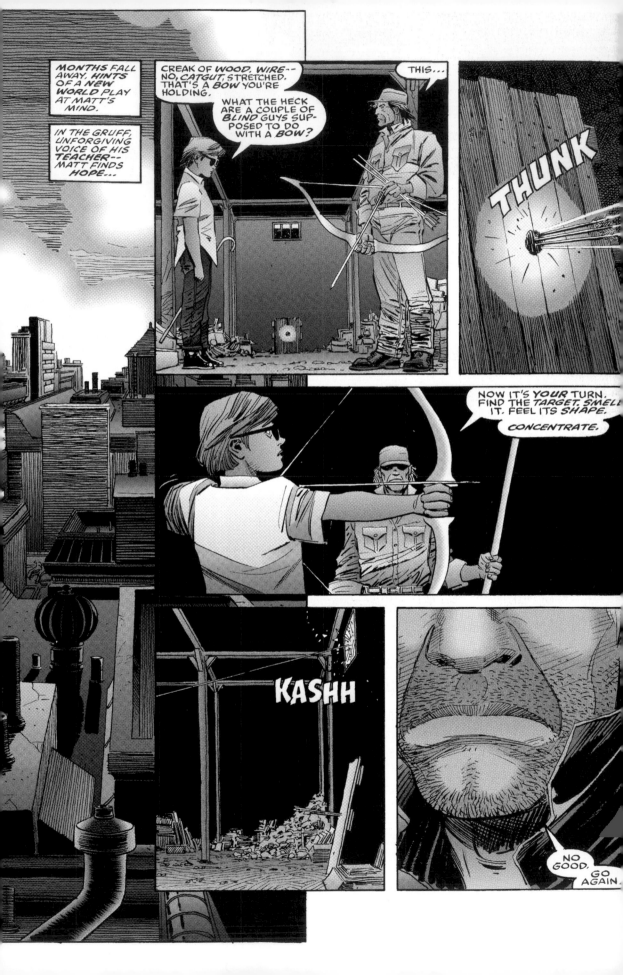

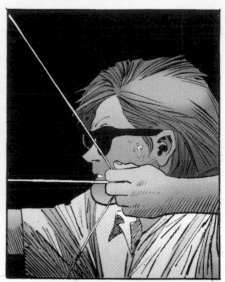

THE NIGHTS ARE THE BEST.

WHEN MATT WAKES BEFORE DAWN--AND, AS ALWAYS, STICK IS THERE--

--AND THEY DANCE, UNSEEN...

CENTRAL PARK. A SPRING MORNING.

JACK MURDOCK JOGS. A FIGHTER HAS TO KEEP IN SHAPE.

A FIGHTER...HE FEELS LIKE A FIGHTER AGAIN.

SIX VICTORIES IN A ROW. SIX KNOCKOUTS. AT HIS AGE, IT'S IMPOSSIBLE BUT THERE IT IS--

--AND NOW HE'S SET FOR A BOUT AT MADISON SQUARE GARDEN.

HE FEELS YOUNG AGAIN.

LIFE IS GOOD AGAIN.

AND BEST OF ALL, HE HASN'T GOTTEN ORDERS FROM THE FIXER IN MONTHS...

YOU'RE PUSHING YOURSELF TOO HARD, MURDOCK. YOU'RE NOT A YOUNG MAN ANYMORE.

I HAVEN'T BEEN DOING SO BAD, FIXER.

OH, COME NOW. ARE YOU SO THICK YOU THINK YOU EARNED THOSE KNOCKOUTS? WHY DO YOU THINK THEY CALL ME THE FIXER?

YOU'RE A SET-UP, OLD MAN. I'VE MADE YOU FLAVOR OF THE MONTH IN THE BOXING WORLD. AND YOU'RE GOING TO MAKE ME A BUNDLE OF MONEY--

--WHEN YOU THROW TO-MORROW'S FIGHT.

NO ARGUMENTS, MURDOCK. THE USUAL THREATS APPLY.

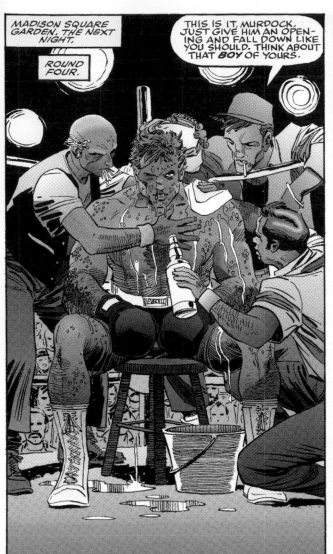

LATER,

JACK MURDOCK EXITS THE STADIUM.

STRANGELY CALM.

READY FOR WHAT'S COMING.

I KNOW YOU'RE THERE. GET IT OVER WITH.

THEY TAKE THEIR TIME,

UNTIL THE SOUNDS ARE WET AND THE PULPY THING THAT WAS ONCE A MAN SAGS, NOT FEELING IT.

MURDOCK STILL STARES ON, CONSCIOUS, BEYOND CARING.

AT THE END, THROUGH THE BLOOD, TOOTHLESS, HE THROWS THE FIXER A YOUNG MAN'S GRIN.

AT THE END, IT'S A MERCY.

BLAM

AT THE MORGUE, AFTER MATT IS FINISHED PLAYING DUMB TO THE COPS, PRETENDING HE DOESN'T KNOW THE WHO OR WHY OF HIS FATHER'S DEATH--

--THE CORONER LETS MATT TOUCH THE CORPSE.

IT'S COLD, ICY COLD.

BUT NOT AS COLD AS THE THING THAT GROWS IN MATT'S BELLY.

HE SPIED ON HIS FATHER. HE KNOWS WHAT JACK MURDOCK DID TO PROTECT AND PROVIDE FOR HIS SON.

AND HE KNOWS THE SMELLS AND SOUNDS OF THE KILLERS.

AND HE KNOWS THEIR NAMES.

McHALE.

GILLIAN.

THE FIRST TWO.

SO I TOLD THAT DAME...

HORAN LIQUORS

...I TOLD HER GOOD...

...HEY, PASS IT OVER, WILL YOU?

GLUB

TAP

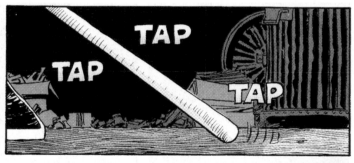

TAP

TAP

TAP

DRINK UP, BOYS. IT'LL HELP WITH THE PAIN.

WHAT THE HELL?

WHO'S DUMB ENOUGH TO MESS WITH US?

IN THE GYM.

THE NEXT TWO.

THE BIG ONE--SLADE--

--WHOSE FISTS SPLINTERED JACK MURDOCK'S JAW AND RIBS--

--SLADE--

--AND SLICK LITTLE MARCELLO, WHO LAUGHED AS HE CARVED UP MURDOCK'S FACE.

ALL MATT HAS TO DO IS THROW A CIRCUIT BREAKER--

--AND THEY'RE AS BLIND AS HE IS.

HEY! WHAT HAPPENED WITH THE LIGHTS?

I CAN'T STAND IT WHEN IT'S DARK...

AW, MARCELLO, YOU WIMP--

WHUDD WHUDD

WHAT THE HELL--

MARCELLO-- WHERE ARE Y--OOF!

AT THE DOOR--SUDDEN RASPY *INTAKE* OF BREATH TO LUNGS THAT ARE *WEAK* FROM DECADES OF ABUSE.

AND THE SCENT OF *TOBACCO* MIXED WITH EX-PENSIVE *AFTER-SHAVE*.

THE FIXER.

LET HIM RUN--

KRY KK

--UNTIL MATT'S FINISHED TURN-ING RIBS INTO BROKEN, *JAGGED* THINGS...

...NOW-- PICK UP THE SOUNDS--

--CLATTER OF FLEEING FOOTSTEPS--

--AWKWARD, PAINFUL *SUCKING* OF AIR--

--A POUNDING, POUNDING HEART--

GYM

ANGELO! GET US OUT OF HERE! NOW!

SCREEEE

ANGELO, AND THE FIXER.

THE LAST TWO.

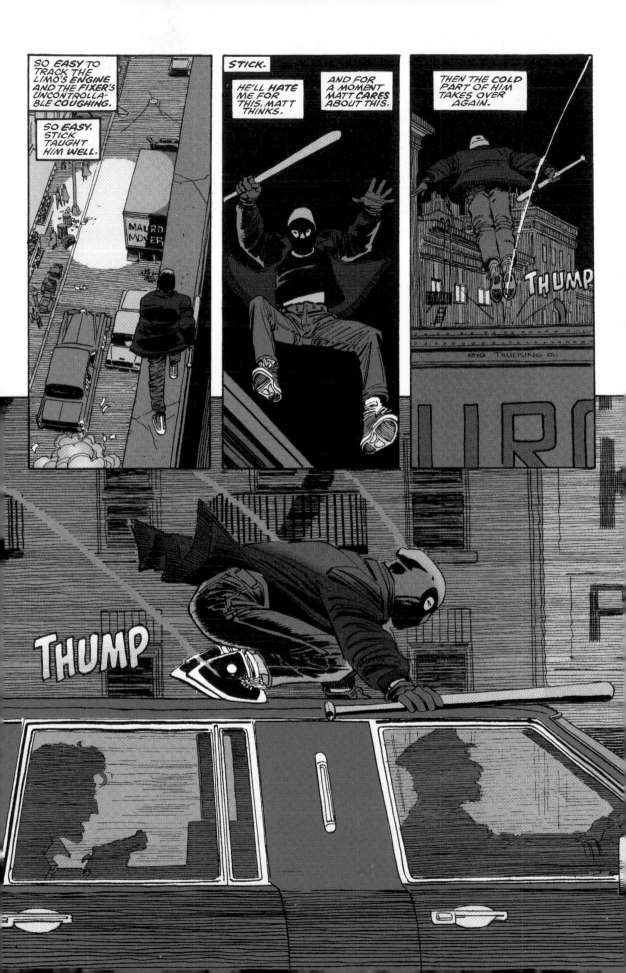

KRESHH

YAAA

MATT'S SKULL STRIKES PAVEMENT--

--A LOST MOMENT--

--THEN THE FOOTSTEPS.

HEADING TO THE SUBWAY.

MATT IGNORES THE DIZZINESS AND THE STICKY SALTY TASTE OF HIS OWN BLOOD--

--AND FOLLOWS THE FIXER'S HEARTBEAT--

--IT'S SO FAST-- SO WEAK--

--AND HE'S COUGHING AGAIN--

--THEN A HORRID HORN BLAST AND AN UNHOLY ROAR-- A TRAIN--

--DEAFENING--

--DEAFENING--

--DEAFENING--

--MATT CAN ONLY STRAIN TO KEEP HIS FEET BENEATH HIM UNTIL IT PASSES...

...THEN--A SOUND MADE OF OIL AND STEEL--

--A REVOLVER, COCKED--

--AND THAT BREATHING--THAT HEARTBEAT--

--THAT HEARTBEAT--

--POUNDING--

--FLUTTERING--

--STOPPING--

THE FIXER SLUMPS TO THE FLOOR WITH A SIGH AND BREATHES HIS LAST PATHETIC BREATH AND MATT IS ALONE IN THE STATION.

ALONE, BUT NOT FINISHED.

ONE REMAINS.

ANGELO.

MEANWHILE, IN A HOSPITAL...

...AND MURDOCK, HE COULD *SEE IN THE DARK*-- AND HE HAD *SIX ARMS!*

MURDOCK'S LYING INNA MORGUE WITH TWO ARMS AND A TAG ON HIS TOE, BUDDY.

IT'S A *GHOST*, LIEUTENANT! IT WAS *HIM!* IT WAS *MURDOCK!*

SO EITHER WE GOT US A *GHOST* OR YOUSE GUYS BEEN HITTING THE *SAUCE* TOO HARD OR WE GOT US A *VIGILANTE.*

ME, I'M BETTING ON THE *SAUCE.*

ONE REMAINS.

ANGELO.

HE THINKS HE'S ESCAPED.

ESCAPED TO A PLACE OF THICK *PERFUMES* AND PRACTICED *PASSION.*

THEY KNOW HIM HERE. HE THINKS HE'S SAFE.

JUST *RELAX*, ANGELO. WE'LL TAKE CARE OF YOU.

IT WAS SOME KIND OF *CRAZY MAN*--

--OUT OF *NOWHERE* HE--

AAAA

IT'S A *RAID!*

BUT WE'RE *PAID UP!*

THAT'S NO COP! *KILL HIM!*

A TANGLE OF FLESH--

--CHOKING PERFUME--

--FISTS AND FINGERNAILS AND CURSES AND SHOUTS--

--TOO MUCH--

--MATT THRASHES--

AAAA

KASHH

OH PLEASE NO...

SHE DOESN'T SCREAM.

SHE PRAYS TO GOD.

AND THEN THERE IS THE CRUNCH OF BONE AND THE SPLATTER OF BLOOD ACROSS PAVEMENT.

NO...

...NO...

...NO!

SHE'S DEAD!

HE KILLED HER!

HE DIDN'T EVEN KNOW HER AND HE KILLED HER!

HE RUNS, HELP-LESS, IN HORROR.

HE RUNS TO THE BASEMENT SEEKING HIS TEACHER--NOT FINDING HIM--

-- HE RUNS TO THE GYM -- HE SCREAMS THE NAME --

STICK!

STICK!

HE SCREAMS UNTIL HIS VOICE IS *HOARSE* AND *CROAKING* AND HIS THROAT IS FULL OF *SAND.*

STICK...

BUT THERE IS NO ANSWER.

STICK...

BLOCKS AWAY...

YOU MUST *RECONSIDER*, STICK. THE BOY HAS *TALENT*.

NO. I WAS *WRONG* ABOUT HIM.

YOU'VE *SAID* IT *YOURSELF*-- A *THOUSAND* TIMES. WE NEED ALL THE HELP WE CAN GET.

HE IS *UN-DISCIPLINED*. *EMOTIONAL*. JUST *LOOK* AT WHAT HE DID TONIGHT!

STICK...WE ARE ALL THAT STANDS BETWEEN THE WORLD AND FORCES OF MYSTIC *DARKNESS*--AND WE GROW *OLD*. WE NEED *YOUNG BLOOD*, YOUNG *STRENGTH*.

IN THIS *GENERATION*, ONLY *TWO ADEPTS* HAVE BEEN BORN. *MATT MURDOCK*-- AND THE GIRL *ELEKTRA*. AND *ALREADY* THE GIRL HAS BEEN *INFECTED* WITH THE DARK WAYS. SHE COULD WELL END UP *RECRUITED* BY THE ENEMY...

...*MATT MURDOCK* MUST GET *ONE MORE CHANCE!* ONE MORE *TEST!*

THAT IS *ENOUGH*, STONE. NO MORE *DISCUSSION*. WE CAN'T LET OUR ORDER BE *COMPROMISED*.

THE BOY HAS *FAILED*. HE IS *USELESS* TO US.

COLUMBIA UNIVERSITY.
ONE YEAR LATER.

HONK
HONK

HUFF
HUFF

HONK

MOVE IT, FATSO!

HUFF

THIS IS FRANKLIN NELSON, FRESHMAN STUDENT OF LAW. HIS FRIENDS CALL HIM "FOGGY".

STEP IT UP, YOU TUB OF LARD!

HA HA HA HA

HONK

THESE BOYS ARE NOT HIS FRIENDS.

LATER, AT THE DORMITORY, FOGGY CONFERS WITH HIS ROOM-MATE...

IT WAS BRAD AGAIN, MATT.

...FELLOW FRESHMAN MATT MURDOCK.

I'VE NEVER DONE ANYTHING TO HIM!

I'M SURE YOU HAVEN'T, FOGGY.

I'M SURE THERE'S NO REASON FOR IT.

BULLIES NEVER NEED A REASON.

THE NEXT DAY.

BRAD JUST WON'T LET UP.

YOU BE *CAREFUL* WALKING BACK TO THE *DORM* TONIGHT, *FAT BOY*--

--NO *TELLING* WHAT COULD *HAPPEN.*

AW, *LAY OFF,* WILL YOU, BRAD?

I'M NOT TAKING ANY *ORDERS* FROM ANY *BLIMPS* TODAY, NELSON.

IT ISN'T UNTIL THAT *MORNING* THAT ANYBODY HEARS THE MUFFLED *SOBS.*

BRAD'S HAD A LONG NIGHT TO THINK IT OVER. TO RE-MEMBER THE STRONG *HANDS* THAT LIFTED HIM FROM HIS BED LIKE HE WAS A *DOLL*--

--THAT CARRIED HIM ACROSS CAMPUS *ROOFTOPS*--

--THAT *HELD HIM,* BY THE *HANDS,* DANGLING HIGH ABOVE CRUEL PAVEMENT...

BRAD'S HAD A LONG NIGHT TO REMEMBER THE *HANDS*-- AND THE *VOICE.*

THE *VOICE* CHILLED HIM MORE THAN THE WINTER COLD.

THE *VOICE* TOLD HIM THIS WAS JUST A *WARNING.*

THE *VOICE* TOLD HIM IN GREAT *DETAIL* WHAT WOULD HAPPEN TO HIM IF BRAD WAS ANYTHING BUT *EXTREMELY PLEASANT* TO *FOGGY NELSON.*

BY THE TIME THEY *COME* FOR HIM--

--BRAD IS A *CHANGED* MAN.

OR, AT LEAST--

--HE IS A *BOY* WHO HAS BEEN TAUGHT A *STERN LESSON.*

AND SO...

I DON'T KNOW WHAT TO DO, MATT! I CAN'T *THINK* STRAIGHT!

EVEN WHEN BRAD *DOESN'T* COME AFTER ME I'M ALL TIED UP IN *KNOTS!*

I'M SURE EVERYTHING WILL WORK ITSELF OUT, FOGGY.

A LOT *YOU* KNOW...

OH, MAN. HERE HE COMES *NOW.*

EXCUSE ME, NELSON. MAY I HAVE A WORD WITH YOU?

UH... SURE, BRAD. WHAT'S UP?

HEY-- CHECK THIS OUT.

I JUST WANT YOU TO KNOW I'M *REALLY SORRY* I'VE BEEN *RIDING* YOU SO HARD. I'VE REALLY BEEN A *JERK.*

DID YOU *HEAR* THAT?

WHAT'S WITH *BRAD?*

IF THERE'S ANY WAY I CAN MAKE GOOD WITH YOU, YOU JUST LET ME KNOW. YOU'RE *OKAY* IN MY BOOK, FOGGY--

-- IT'S OKAY IF I CALL YOU *FOGGY,* ISN'T IT?

SURE, BRAD. IT'S FINE.

GET A LOAD OF *THAT!* YOU SHOULD'VE SEEN HIS *FACE,* MATT!

I WISH I COULD HAVE, FOGGY. I DEARLY WISH I COULD HAVE SEEN HIS FACE.

MATT?

HI, IT'S ME--*CATHY*. FROM OLD MAN *LYNCH*'S CLASS. I WAS JUST WONDERING IF YOU COULD HELP ME *OUT*, WITH THE *EXAM* I MEAN.

I'M A LITTLE *CONFUSED* ON THAT *STOELTING VS. WEST* DECISION...

I'M SORRY, CATHY.

SHE ISN'T CON-FUSED. SHE DOESN'T NEED HIS *HELP* IN HER *STUDIES*--

I CAN'T HELP YOU. I'M LATE FOR CLASS.

--AND HE CAN'T ALLOW HIMSELF TO *RESPOND* TO HER. HE CAN'T ALLOW HIMSELF *EMOTION*.

THAT MUCH, HE HAS *LEARNED*. THE COST IS TOO GREAT.

SIGH...

WHAT A *CREEP*!

OH, HE'S NOT SO BAD.

HE'S JUST REALLY *INTENSE*.

ANOTHER NIGHT FALLS.

AND ONCE AGAIN MATT MURDOCK FINDS HIM-SELF COMING *ALIVE* JUST WHEN HE SHOULD BE GETTING *SLEEPY*.

SPACE... THE *FINAL* FRONTIER...

...THESE ARE THE VOYAGES...

...ITS FIVE YEAR MISSION...

...TO BOLDLY GO *KLIK*

IT WASN'T JUST THE *TELEVISION* THAT KEPT MATT AWAKE.

ZZZZ NNKK

FOGGY'S *SNORING* COULD RAISE THE *DEAD.*

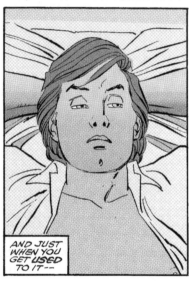

AND JUST WHEN YOU GET *USED* TO IT--

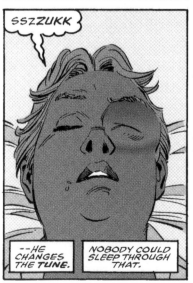

SSZZUKK

--HE CHANGES THE *TUNE.*

NOBODY COULD SLEEP THROUGH THAT.

NO, NO USE KIDDING HIMSELF.

ZERKK

IT'S NOT THE SNORING.

IT'S NOTHING INSIDE THE ROOM.

IT'S OUTSIDE. EVERYWHERE OUTSIDE.

IT'S THE WIND--

--AND EVERYTHING IT CARRIES--

--EVERYTHING IT TOUCHES.

IT CHARGES OFF THE OCEAN, FIERCE, BITTER COLD.

IT RATTLES ANTENNAE AND SHAKES POWER LINES AND LEAVES SWIRLING SNOW IN ITS WAKE--

--IT ROARS DOWN CONCRETE CANYONS--

--AND BRITTLE BRANCHES CLATTER IN COMBAT--

--SURRENDERING WINTER LEAVES THAT RUSTLE AND SKITTER LIKE FAIRIES, BEGGING MATT TO JOIN IN THE DANCE...

...THE CITY NEVER SLEEPS!

DOWN THE STREET-- WARMTH AND KINDNESS TO A SHIVERING SOUL...

GOD BLESS YOU, MAN.

...MUSIC FROM CAR RADIOS--IN A HUNDRED DIFFERENT LANGUAGES--

--DOGS YIP AND BARK AND WHINE--

--ONE HOWLS-- CELEBRATING THE NIGHT...

A SCENT-- HUMAN AND FRAGRANT--

--UP HERE?

YES-- AND NOW A BREATH.

ANOTHER.

NEARBY.

A PULSE, STRONG, STEADY--

--MOVING ACROSS THE ROOFTOPS, AGAINST THE WIND, DEFIANT--

--FOOTSTEPS LIGHT AS A CAT'S--

--OVER THERE--

--THAT SCENT AGAIN--

--NOT A MAN'S SCENT--

--FALLING NOW--

--CRAZY--

--SHE'S FALLING--

...HE LOCKS ON THE SCENT, THE TANTALIZING SOUNDS.

HE CAN'T LOSE HER NOW.

HE'LL CATCH HER AND FIND OUT WHO SHE IS--

--PROVIDED THIS BLIND MAN CAN CROSS THE STREET.

KEKK

NFF

SPLAT

OWW!

HELP!

SOMEBODY HELP!

AND NOW A BLOOD-CHILLING SCREAM--

--FOLLOWED BY ANOTHER CHUCKLE--

--AND HER SCENT--

--CLINGING TO RUBBER AND CLOTH.

A TRAIL.

QUITE A TRAIL.

THE NEXT DAY. ON CAMPUS.

I DON'T KNOW HOW YOU *DO* IT, MATT. HERE I STUDY TILL I'M *POOPED* TO MAKE THE GRADE--

--AND YOU JUST SEEM TO BREEZE *THROUGH*!

MAYBE YOU SHOULDN'T HAVE THAT *TV* ON WHEN YOU HIT THE *BOOKS*, FOGGY.

HEY, LET'S NOT GET *RADICAL*, BUDDY.

HOLD IT.

SCREEECH!

YIKES!

WHAT ARE YOU *GRINNING* ABOUT? YOU COULD HAVE *HIT* US!

MATT-- WHAT--

--WHAT ARE YOU *DOING*?!

AWAY ZONE

VROOOM

MATT?

SOMETIMES YOU'RE KIND OF HARD TO FIGURE OUT, PAL.

NINETY-FIVE IN THE SNOW.

HER DRIVING WOULD SCARE ANYBODY.

IT'S BEEN SO LONG SINCE MATT HAD A GOOD SCARE.

SCREECH

HONK

LUNATIC!

KUMP

HE TELLS HIMSELF HE SHOULDN'T ENJOY THIS.

AND NOW THE AIR GOES THIN--MOUNTAIN AIR, THE KIND THAT MAKES YOUR HEAD GO LIGHT.

SNOW STABS AT EXPOSED SKIN-- PAINFUL, BRACING.

EXCUSE ME, MISS--

--BUT PERHAPS YOU SHOULD PUT THE TOP UP.

WHY?

HAHAHAHA HAHAHAHA HAHA

VROOOO

LATER. BACK AT THE DORM.

MATT?

WOAH, MATT. WHAT HAPPENED?

I WENT SWIMMING.

SWIMMING. RIGHT. WITH THAT *ELEKTRA* GIRL.

SHE'S *BAD NEWS*, MATT.

YOU KNOW FLINT'S *SKIING ACCIDENT?* THE ONE WHERE HE BROKE *BOTH* HIS *ARMS?* WELL, YOU DIDN'T HEAR IT FROM *ME,* BUT HE DIDN'T GET HURT *SKIING.*

BUZZ TOLD ME FLINT MADE A *PASS* AT ELEKTRA. AND BEFORE YOU *KNEW* IT SHE WAS *LAUGHING* AND THERE HE WAS...

ELEKTRA.

ELEKTRA. WHERE DOES SHE LIVE?

FOGGY KNOWS BETTER THAN TO ARGUE WHEN MATT'S LIKE THIS.

AND SO, AT A *RESIDENCE* OUTSIDE OF TOWN...

...A VERY *WELL-GUARDED* RESIDENCE...

...MATT MAKES HIS *MOVE.*

REMEMBER WHAT *STICK* TAUGHT YOU, HE TELLS HIMSELF.

YOUR RIBS CAN *FLEX.*

LET THEM.

MAKE NO *SOUND.*

THERE ARE TIMES WHEN MATT *IS GLAD* TO BE BLIND.

PEOPLE DEPEND ON THEIR *EYES* FOR ALMOST *EVERYTHING.*

THEY MISS SO *MUCH.*

HE GIVES HIMSELF A MOMENT TO LET THE *AIR* AND THE *SMELLS* AND THE ECHOING *SOUNDS* DESCRIBE THE PLACE.

QUITE A *SPREAD.*

FOGGY SAID ELEKTRA'S *FATHER* IS SOME KIND OF BIG SHOT DIPLOMAT. A *POWERFUL* MAN.

SHE'S PROB-ABLY HAD IT *EASY* ALL HER LIFE.

SHE COULD USE A *LESSON--*

--A LESSON THIS BOY FROM THE TENEMENTS OF HELL'S KITCHEN IS READY TO *TEACH.*

SHE'S NOT *RIGHT* ABOUT MATT, EITHER. HE'S *NOT A WILD MAN.*

HE CAN *CONTROL* THAT PART OF HIMSELF, THAT CHILDISH MISCHIEF-MAKER, THAT *DAREDEVIL...*

...THIS, HE THINKS, AS HE MOVES WITH SMOOTH SKILL THAT WOULD PUT A *CAT BURGLAR* TO SHAME.

HER SCENT.

HER ROOM.

HE SOAKS IT IN. LINGERING HERE, THEN THERE, HIS *SENSES* PROBING, PROBING.

IT IS AN ACT AS INTIMATE AS IF HE WERE RUNNING HIS HANDS OVER HER BODY...

...SO MANY *TROPHIES*.

SWIMMING. TRACK.

AIKIDO. KENDO. KARATE.

FIRST PRIZE, EVERY TIME.

DADDY'S LITTLE GIRL CAN *FIGHT*.

NOTHING MORE TO FIND HERE...

WAIT.

A DOG COMING.

NO PROBLEM.

DOGS ALWAYS LOVE MATT.

...PIANO MUSIC, SOMETHING CLASSICAL-- AND VERY, VERY DIFFICULT.

BUT SHE MAKES IT SOUND EASY.

IS THERE ANYTHING SHE'S BAD AT?

AND NOW SHATTERING GLASS, A SMALL SOUND--

--IN A VERY BIG ROOM.

KASHH

SIR, I'M *GETTING SOMETHING* FROM THE *GATE.* THE SUBJECT HAS *ESCAPED*--

--HE USED SOME KIND OF *KARATE* MOVE ON *POULOS*-- BUT POULOS GOT A *SHOT* OFF. TAGGED HIM IN THE *ARM.*

HE MUST BE *BLEEDING.*

YES, MISS. HE'S *LOSING A LOT OF BLOOD.* HE WON'T GET *FAR.*

MATT DOES *GET FAR.*

MATT GETS *ALL THE WAY BACK INTO TOWN.*

HE CAN'T RE- MEMBER *HOW.*

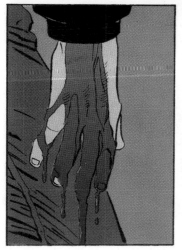

HIS *SENSES* COME AND GO.

HE HAS NO IDEA HOW MANY TIMES HE *FALLS.*

HE CRAWLS DEEP INSIDE HIMSELF.

THROUGH WAVES OF NAUSEA AND CLAMMY, ICY COLD, HE CONCENTRATES--

--CONCENTRATES--

-- AND HE FINDS THE STRENGTH HE NEEDS.

TO MAKE IT BACK.

TO THE DORM.

CLEAN THE WOUND.

STOP THE BLEEDING.

STAY CONSCIOUS.

STAY CONSCIOUS.

IT'S SIMPLE. SIMPLE.

DON'T GO INTO SHOCK.
CLEAN THE WOUND.
STAY CONSCIOUS.
STOP THE BLEEDING.
STAY CONSCIOUS.

IGNORE THE PAIN.

STAY CONSCIOUS.

THEN THE BLEEDING STOPS AND, LIGHT-HEADED, HE KNOWS HE WILL LIVE.

HE LETS THE OUTSIDE WORLD BACK IN...

...TO FEEL STEAM--

--AND HEAR THE RUSH OF WATER, THE SHOWER.

HE'S NOT ALONE.

AND IT'S NOT FOGGY...

SO. UM.
MATT. UM.

ELEKTRA,
HUH?

SHE'S
REALLY
A VERY
NICE GIRL,
FOGGY.

SHE WENT **HOME** AND TRIED TO GET SOME **SLEEP** BUT THE **VOICES** STARTED IN AGAIN AND THEY WOULDN'T STOP.

SHE COULDN'T STAND TO BE INSIDE.

SHE'S DRAWN **BACK TO TIMES SQUARE**--

--TO THE **CORNER** WHERE THE ONES SHE'S **WATCHED** STAND, LEERING AND SNICKERING,

SHE'S HEARD THEM **BRAG** ABOUT WHAT THEY'VE **DONE TO INNOCENT WOMEN.**

AND, FEELING **RESTLESS**--

--SHE LETS THEM **SEE** HER, THIS TIME.

THEY ARE PIGS. VERMIN. LISTEN TO THEM CHATTER.

BUILDING THEIR COURAGE.

THEY DESERVE WHAT'S COMING.

THIS IS THE BEST SHE CAN DO, OBEYING THE URGE--

--BUT NOT THE VOICES.

SHE'S NOT CRAZY. THE VOICES ARE REAL.

SHE MADE THE MISTAKE OF TELLING POPPA ABOUT THEM, ONCE.

THEN CAME THE PSYCHIATRISTS. THEY ALL MISSED THE POINT.

SHE HAD TO LIE TO GET RID OF THE PSYCHIATRISTS AND ALL THEIR STUPID QUESTIONS.

THE VOICES ARE REAL.

THAT'S FAR ENOUGH, BABE.

YOU CAN SCREAM IF YOU WANT TO.

I WON'T SCREAM.

LET THEM WATCH.

LET THEM BREATHE HARD.

LET THEM ENJOY THEMSELVES-- WHILE THEY CAN.

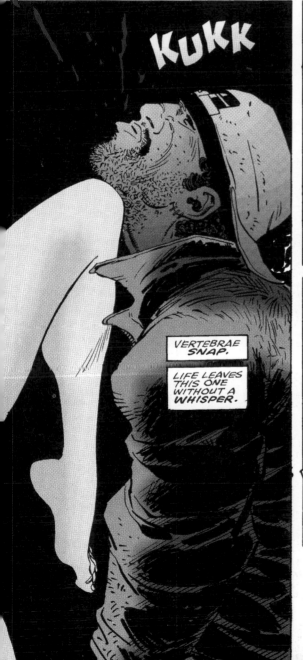

BUT HE'S JUST *BIG* AND *STRONG* AND *STUPID.*

HER *FOOT* CUTS THROUGH THE *MEAT* OF HIM LIKE A *KNIFE*...

ONLY HIS *WEAPON* IS OF ANY *USE.*

...IF *POPPA* COULD *SEE* THIS HE WOULD *NEVER* FOR-GIVE HER...

...THE ONE WITH THE *GUN.*

MORE *RUDE* LANGUAGE.

SHE'S STILL *CURSING* AS THE CHAIN TURNS HER *WRIST* TO PULP.

THEN IT'S A SIMPLE MATTER OF SHOVING SHARP BONE INTO SOFT BRAIN.

A NOVICE COULD DO IT.

ONLY THE BIG ONE REMAINS.

ELEKTRA HATES THE SMELL OF HIS SWEAT.

CH!NG

SNAP

A FEW LAST GURGLING SOUNDS AND THE ALLEY GOES QUIET.

IT TAKES THE POLICE A FULL TWENTY MINUTES TO ARRIVE.

ELEKTRA HAILS A CAB.

OH, BROTHER-- WHAT A MESS!

WHATTAYAMEAN YOU DIDN'T SEE NOTHING?

I WAS DRUNK!

MAN, WE GOT FIVE DEAD HERE!

I WAS DRUNK!

LOOK AT THIS. WHOEVER ACED THESE GUYS GOT ONE DAMN STRANGE SENSE OF HUMOR.

IT WAS A DIS-APPOINTING WORKOUT.

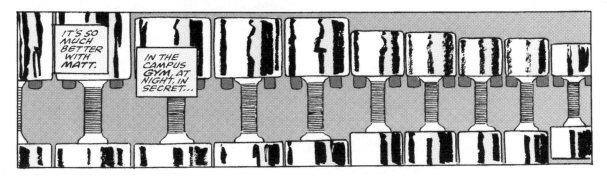

IT'S SO MUCH BETTER WITH MATT.

IN THE CAMPUS GYM, AT NIGHT, IN SECRET...

--THE ONLY TIMES SHE IS NOT *LONELY*--

--ARE THE TIMES SHE SPENDS WITH *MATT.*

SHE KNOWS IT CANNOT *LAST.*

BUT FOR NOW, THEIR *SWEAT* MIXED, THEIR *BODIES* AND *HEARTS* AS *ONE*--

--SHE IS *HAPPY.*

AND SO IS *MATT.*

PERHAPS A LITTLE *TOO* HAPPY.

BUT THAT'S *HIS* PROBLEM.

MISTER *MURDOCK?*

I ASKED YOU A *QUESTION,* MISTER MURDOCK.

MURDOCK-- ARE YOU *LISTENING?*

MATT. I THINK YOU'D BETTER *ANSWER* HIM...

THAT NIGHT. AT THE DORM.

A SURPRISE VISIT.

STAY AWAY FROM HER, KID.

HNH?...

...STICK-- WHAT--

HUKK

ZURK

SHUT UP AND LISTEN. THAT GIRL IS POISON. SHE'S ON HER WAY TO THE WORST SIDE AND SHE'LL DRAG YOU DOWN WITH HER.

IT'S BAD ENOUGH YOU FAILED ME. I WON'T HAVE YOU JOINING THE ENEMY. I'LL KILL YOU FIRST.

SO STAY AWAY FROM ELEKTRA.

YOU CAN'T TELL ME WHAT--

HHUURGG

A JAB AT HIS THROAT--

--AND THE WORLD GOES WHITE AND SILENT.

AND WHEN HE WAKES, MATT CAN ONLY WONDER-- WAS IT A DREAM?

YES. IT HAD TO BE A DREAM. HOW COULD ELEKTRA BE EVIL?...

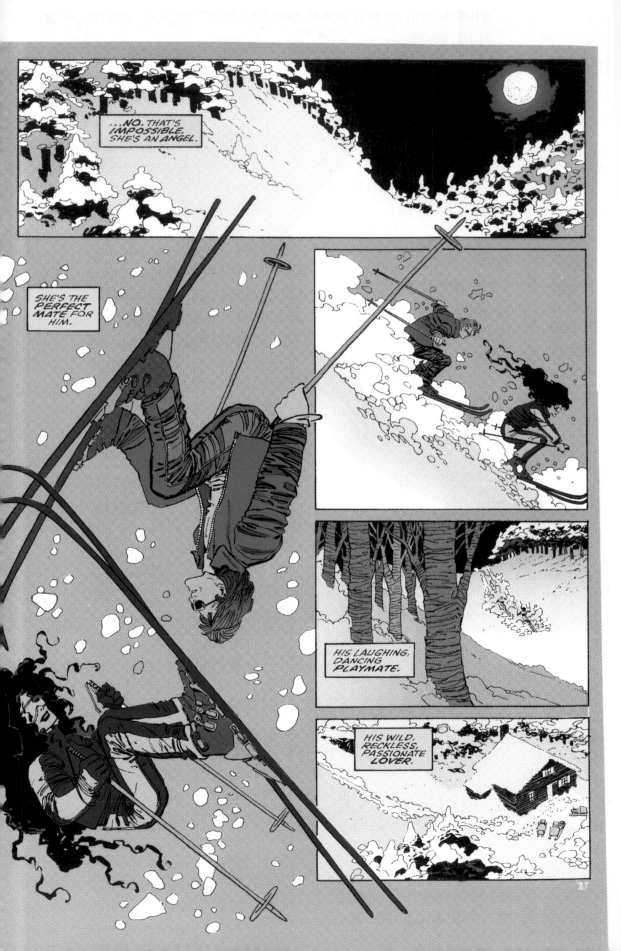

BUT WHEN HE HINTS AT THEIR *FUTURE* TOGETHER, HER LAUGH IS DARK AND TERRIBLY *SAD*...

YOU NEVER ASK ME ANY *QUESTIONS*, MATT. YOU DON'T REALLY KNOW ME.

YOU'RE SOMETHING I DON'T *DESERVE.* SOMETHING I CAN'T *KEEP.*

IF I COULD HAVE *STOPPED* MYSELF, I NEVER WOULD'VE COME TO YOU. IT WAS WRONG.

YOU'RE EVERYTHING I NEED, ELEKTRA. EVERYTHING I'VE EVER WANTED.

I KILLED FIVE MEN LAST WEEK.

ACTUALLY, ONE OF THEM WAS A WOMAN.

DON'T TALK CRAZY.

NO. OF COURSE YOU CAN'T BELIEVE ME.

I'M TIRED.

AND, LIKE A CAT--

--SHE SLEEPS.

I LOVE YOU, ELEKTRA.

MATT'S OLD NEIGHBOR-HOOD, HELL'S KITCHEN.

A SUMMIT CONFERENCE--

--OF THE LEADERS OF THE MANHATTAN UNDERWORLD.

TIMES *CHANGE*, RIGOLETTO. WE GOT *STREET KIDS* OUT THERE *COMPETING* WITH US.

COMPETING, HELL. THEY'RE LEAVING US IN THE *DUST*--BE-CAUSE THEY *KNOW* WHAT PEOPLE *WANT*.

PLEASE LISTEN TO THEM, UNCLE. PROFITS ARE *DOWN*--

ENOUGH! I'LL HEAR NO *MORE* OF THIS!

BE *REASONABLE*, BOSS. WE'VE ALL GOT *FAMILIES* TO THINK OF, AND *EMPLOYEES*.

WHY THE SUDDEN *MORALITY*, RIGO-LETTO? *MONEY* IS THERE TO BE *MADE* --AND I'M TALKING *BILLIONS*. WHY LET SMALL TIME *PIMPS* AND *PUSHERS* CLEAN UP, WHEN WE HAVE THE *MACHINERY* IN PLACE TO DO IT *OUR-SELVES?*

SHUT UP! ALL OF YOU! WE WILL NOT MURDER *CHILDREN!* WE WILL NOT *CATER* TO UNHOLY *PER-VERSIONS!* WE WILL NOT *INFECT* OUR NEIGHBORHOODS WITH *CRACK COCAINE!* WE STICK TO THE *OLD RACKETS!* WE MAY BE *CRIMINALS,* BUT WE ARE NOT *MONSTERS!*

NOW GET OUT OF HERE! ALL OF YOU!

OH, MY FRIEND, MY FRIEND... THEY EXHAUST ME. THEY WOULD SELL *AWAY* OUR *TRADITIONS*-- OUR *HONOR*. OUR OWN *FAMILIES* LIVE IN THIS CITY-- AND THEY WOULD TURN IT INTO HELL ON EARTH...

MY FRIEND, I NEED YOUR *HANDS*...

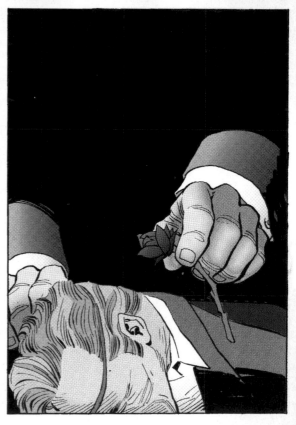

HE HAS WAITED FOR *YEARS*, THIS KILLER. QUIETLY MAKING THE PROPER CONNECTIONS. BUILDING A SILENT CONSENSUS.

SOON THAT CONSENSUS WILL BE AN UNSHAKABLE *STRANGLEHOLD*. THEY WILL OBEY HIM OR *DIE*.

HE WILL *RULE* THIS CITY.

AS THE LORD OF CRIME.

THE KINGPIN.

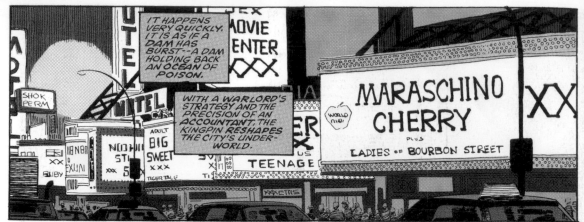

IT HAPPENS VERY QUICKLY. IT IS AS IF A DAM HAS BURST--A DAM HOLDING BACK AN OCEAN OF POISON.

WITH A WARLORD'S STRATEGY AND THE PRECISION OF AN ACCOUNTANT, THE KINGPIN RESHAPES THE CITY'S UNDERWORLD.

AND THE PROFITS ROLL IN. BY THE BILLIONS.

PROFITS--FROM THE KIDNAPPING AND OUTRIGHT SALE OF THE CITY'S CHILDREN--

--CONDEMNING INNOCENTS TO FATES THAT ARE UNSPEAKABLE.

PROFITS--FROM STATE OF THE ART DRUGS THAT TURN WORKING CITIZENS INTO HOLLOW HELPLESS WRETCHES WHO WILL DO ANYTHING TO SATISFY A CRAVING THAT WILL NEVER END...

PROFITS--FROM COUNTLESS LIVES RUINED.

FROM COUNTLESS LIVES LOST.

AND ANY IN HIS RANKS WHO LACK THE STOMACH TO OBEY HIM--ANY WHO EXPRESS A MOMENT'S DOUBT--

--ARE SWIFTLY ELIMINATED BY THE KINGPIN'S DEATH SQUAD OF MERCENARIES GATHERED FROM AROUND THE GLOBE--

--HIS PRIVATE GESTAPO.

BUT MOST FEARED OF ALL IS THE SILENT MAN AT THE KINGPIN'S SIDE, THE MAN CALLED *LARKS.*

THE KINGPIN NURTURED HIM, SINCE HE WAS A BOY. TRAINED HIM IN THE MANY WAYS OF *DEATH.*

DROVE HIS *SOUL* FROM HIM.

LEAVING A THING WITH AN ICY MASK FOR A FACE.

A THING TO WHOM *KILLING* IS AS NATURAL AS *BREATHING.*

A THING THAT FINDS PLEASURE ONLY IN COLD *CRUELTY.*

YEARS PASS.

MATT MURDOCK GRADUATES *SUMMA CUM LAUDE* FROM HARVARD LAW SCHOOL AND FINDS WORK AT THE BOSTON FIRM OF SUSSMAN AND CASTRO.

HE IS NOT HAPPY, BUT HE IS BUSY. AND THAT'S CLOSE ENOUGH.

UNTIL THE PAST COMES CALLING.

EXCUSE ME, MURDOCK, BUT I'M NOT *ASKING.*

YOU SHOULD BE GRATEFUL FOR THIS OPPORTUNITY.

YES, SIR.

YOU'VE DONE *GOOD* WORK FOR US, MATT. KEEP IT UP AND YOU'RE ON YOUR WAY TO BECOMING THE YOUNGEST JUNIOR PARTNER WE'VE EVER HAD.

NOW GET YOUR BRIEF ON THAT PLANE TO *NEW YORK* AND NO MORE *ARGUMENTS!*

YES, SIR.

NEW YORK. IT STILL SOUNDS THE SAME, IT STILL FEELS THE SAME.

AND ALL THE MEMORIES SURGE UP, LAUGHING AT HIM LIKE SCHOOLYARD *BULLIES.*

YOU CAN'T ESCAPE ME, THE CITY ROARS.

YOU CAN'T ESCAPE YOURSELF.

AND SO MATT COMES BACK.

HIS MIDTOWN HOTEL ROOM FEELS LIKE A PRISON CELL. NO HARM IN TAKING A SHORT WALK, HE TELLS HIMSELF...

THE SOUNDS AND SMELLS WRAP THEMSELVES AROUND HIM. HE FEELS THE CITY'S HIDDEN PULSE, BEATING IN TIME WITH HIS OWN. HE IGNORES HIS IMMEDIATE SURROUNDINGS, LOST IN IT--

--UNTIL HE SMELLS THE BREAD.

PASCAL'S BAKERY.

HE'S WANDERED TO HELL'S KITCHEN.

AND THE YEARS MELT AWAY.

AND HE CAN HEAR THE RATTLE OF HIS SKATE-BOARD.

THE ANGRY SHOUTS OF OFFICER LIEBOWITZ.

THE SMACK OF DAD'S RIGHT HOOK AND THE RISING CHEER OF THE CROWD.

AND THAT SOUND THAT MADE HIS STOMACH GO COLD.

THE NASTY ELECTRIC BUZZER THAT MEANS RECESS.

RECESS. AND THE NICKNAME.

DAREDEVIL.

AND THE GIRLS GIGGLE AND POINT.

DAREDEVIL.

AND THE BULLIES' FISTS STRIKE HIS BELLY, HIS FACE.

DAREDEVIL.

AND THE CHAIN LINK OF THE FENCE BITES INTO HIS BACK.

DAREDEVIL.

AND THE WHOLE WORLD LAUGHS AT HIM.

DAREDEVIL.

DAREDEVIL.

DAREDEVIL.

AND NOW A NEW VOICE, CREAMY WITH CONFIDENCE.

BLIND MAN--I'M TALKING TO YOU.

WITH A BULLY'S CONFIDENCE.

AND BULLIES NEVER STRIKE ALONE.

LEAVE ME ALONE. I DON'T WANT ANY TROUBLE.

YOU SHOULD'VE THOUGHT ABOUT THAT BEFORE YOU PUT ON THAT THREE HUNDRED DOLLAR SUIT AND WENT CRUISING HELL'S KITCHEN.

IT'S ONE HELL OF A NICE SUIT.

I GET THE SHOES.

GIVE US A SHOW, BLIND MAN. STRIP.

SNIKK

I SAID-- GAA

KRU KK

MATT DOESN'T HEAR THE CURSES.

HE ONLY HEARS THE NAME--

YOU SHOULDN'T HAVE CALLED ME THAT.

NO--

--LEAVE ME ALONE--

BUT THE BULLIES WON'T STOP SAYING IT.

AND THE CHAIN LINK BITES HIS BACK.

AND THE GIRLS GIGGLE AND POINT.

YAA NO-- PLEASE--

CHUDD

KEFF

FINALLY, THE BUZZER SOUNDS AGAIN.

RECESS IS OVER AT LAST.

HE SHOULD FEEL RELIEVED. AVENGED.

BUT HE JUST FEELS LOST AND ALONE AND SICK.

HE GOES TO HIS FAVORITE PLACE.

THE GYM.

NOW BOARDED UP. ABANDONED.

KREEE

BUT IT STILL HOLDS ALL THE DUSTY SWEATY SMELLS.

HE CAN ALMOST HEAR A YOUNG BOY'S FISTS STRIKING A PUNCHING BAG, THE SOUND ECHOING LIKE MACHINE GUN FIRE...

BUT THAT'S ALL *GONE* NOW. *DEAD AND BURIED.* IN THE *PAST.*

BURIED WITH *DAD.*

BURIED WITH MATT'S *SKATE-BOARD* AND *SKI MASK* AND ALL HIS *MISCHIEF.*

HIS *FEVER* BREAKS. HE'S IN *CONTROL* AGAIN. HE CALMS HIS *HEART...*

...AND HEARS *ANOTHER'S* BEAT.

HE GETS HER *SCENT.*

FEMALE. YOUNG. STRONG. SCARED.

SHE'S HOLDING HER *BREATH.*

NOW--SHE'S *MOVING*--

--RUBBER GIVES OUT A *GROAN*--

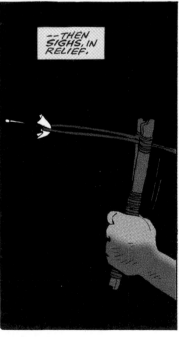

--THEN *SIGHS,* IN *RELIEF.*

I MEAN YOU *NO HARM,* YOUNG LADY.

THPP

NO, IT WAS *DAREDEVIL*.

THEY CALLED ME *DAREDEVIL*.

FAPP

WEEKS SAIL BY, PLEASANTLY ENOUGH.

THEN, ONE DAY, AS MATT PONDERS LUNCH...

YOU WANNA PASTRAMI *REUBEN* ON *WHITE*? THAT'S A DAMN *CRIME*!

AND A SIDE OF *MAYONNAISE*, PLEASE.

MAYO ONNA *REUBEN*? THAT MAKES IT A *FELONY*!

THERE'S NO MISTAKING THE *VOICE*--OR THE *TASTES*.

IT'S FOGGY NELSON-- MATT'S OLD *ROOMMATE*.

IT'S BEEN YEARS. THEY CATCH UP.

...NO BIG COMPLAINTS. THIS CORPO- RATE STUFF MAY BE *BORING*, BUT I'M WORKING WITH A GOOD GROUP. I GUESS I'D *ENJOY* IT MORE IF IT HAD ANYTHING TO DO WITH *PEOPLE*-- DIRECTLY, I MEAN.

PEOPLE, HUH? BOY, I'M *DROWN- ING* IN PEOPLE. A *CLASS ACTION SUIT* AGAINST A *SLUMLORD*. HE WON'T PAY TO KEEP THE PLACE *HEATED* BUT HE'S SPENDING A *FORTUNE* ON HIS *DEFENSE*. HE'S BREAKING MY *BACK*.

HEY, MATT, I HATE TO *ASK*--BUT MY CLIENTS JUST WANT A DECENT PLACE TO *LIVE* --AND YOU WERE ALWAYS SO *CLEVER*...

MATT LEAPS AT THE CHANCE TO HELP. NIGHT AFTER NIGHT, HE RE- SEARCHES AND CON- JECTURES AND POSTULATES--

I THINK I MIGHT HAVE SOMETHING HERE, FOGGY. THE *STOELTING VS. WEST* DECISION. IT'S A *STRETCH*, BUT AN ARGUMENT COULD BE *MADE*... FOGGY?

Z

--AND MATT REMEMBERS *WHY* HE WANTED TO BECOME AN *ATTORNEY*.

TO FIGHT FOR *JUSTICE*.

TO FIGHT THE *BULLIES*.

MEANWHILE, THE BIGGEST *BULLY* IN *TOWN* MAKES HIS FIRST *MISTAKE*.

IT BEGINS WITH A SIMPLE ORDER TO *CUT COSTS* IN THE *FILM DIVISION*.

AFTER *ALL*, THE PRODUCT IS NOT *ART*--AND, FOR ALL THE SCENES OF *PERVERSION* AND *TORTURE* AND *MURDER*--

--THERE IS NO *NEED* FOR *SPECIAL EFFECTS*.

AND SO...

CUT COSTS? WITH THIS PRODUCTION SCHEDULE? HAS THE KINGPIN LOST HIS MIND?

ULP! I NEVER SAID THAT. I NEVER SAID THAT. TELL THE BOSS WE'LL MAKE IT WORK. THAT'S A PROMISE.

SOON. YOU GET ONE CHANCE. YOU BLOW IT AND I NEVER SEE YOU AGAIN. NOBODY DOES. YOU STAY OFF THE JUNK AND YOU GET ME A GIRL. SHE CAN'T BE OLDER THAN TWELVE.

WE'LL DO IT, CLAY. WE'LL DO IT AND WE'LL STAY CLEAN. WE WILL. WE'LL DO IT.

THAT NIGHT.

SYLVIO, THERE SHE IS, I TOLD YOU. EVERY NIGHT SHE HANGS OUT AT THAT OLD GYM. I TOLD YOU.

RIGHT. GREAT. WE'RE ALL SET. GET THE CHLORO-FORM. WE'LL DO IT.

MICKEY'S BUMMED.

MATT'S BEEN TIED UP FOR A WEEK ON SOME DUMB NIGHT JOB AND IT'S NOT AS MUCH FUN WORKING OUT ALONE.

MAYBE SHE DOES HAVE A CRUSH ON HIM. WHY NOT? HE'S HANDSOME AND TALL AND REALLY MYS-TERIOUS.

HE CAN HEAR THINGS NOBODY ELSE CAN. AND HE CAN DO THINGS NOBODY BLIND OUGHT TO BE ABLE TO DO.

HE DOESN'T TALK ABOUT IT AND SHE DOESN'T ASK, BUT IT'S LIKE HE'S GOT MAGIC POWERS OR SOMETHING.

AND SUDDENLY MICKEY MISSES MATT MORE THAN EVER.

DON'T FIGHT ME. DON'T FIGHT ME.

UFF!

OW! SHE BIT ME!

QUICK! GET THAT CHLOROFORM. QUICK.

WOW, THAT STUFF REALLY *WORKS!*

MATT'S HOTEL ROOM.

YES, SIR. THE NEXT FLIGHT OUT.

THEY'RE CALLING ME BACK TO *BOSTON,* FOGGY. THE *WARNER* CASE. SUSSMAN SAYS I LEAVE *TONIGHT*-- OR IT'S MY *JOB.*

AW, HECK. I'M GOING TO *MISS* YOU, BUDDY.

ON THE WAY TO THE AIRPORT.

ONE STOP ON THE WAY, DRIVER. IN HELL'S KITCHEN. IT'S AN OLD *GYM-NASIUM* OFF *COLUMBUS.*

THERE'S SOMEBODY I HAVE TO SAY GOOD-BYE TO.

68

555

BIG A

HE SCANS THE GYM FOR SEVER-AL MINUTES LONGER THAN HE NEEDS.

MICKEY'S NOT THERE.

HE'D HATE TO LEAVE WITHOUT TELLING HER.

SOMETHING *SOFT* HITS MATT'S LEG.

AND SOMETHING *COLD* CRAWLS UP HIS *SPINE.*

IT'S MICKEY'S HAT.

SHE LOVES THAT SILLY OLD HAT.

SHE NEVER TAKES IT OFF.

SHE LOVES IT SO MUCH SHE WROTE HER *NAME* AND *ADDRESS* IN IT.

IN BALLPOINT, LEAVING EASY-TO-READ IMPRESSIONS.

HE CAN *FIND HER.*

HE'LL TAKE A *LATER* FLIGHT-- ONCE HE'S SURE SHE'S *OKAY.*

ACROSS TOWN.

RIGHT, CLAY, RIGHT. YOU'RE THE BOSS...UM, NO, I MEAN SHE'S NOT *EXACTLY* TWELVE...UM, SHE'S *FOURTEEN.* BUT SHE'S KIND OF *SMALL* FOR *FOURTEEN*...NO. YOU'RE *KIDDING,* RIGHT, CLAY?...

CLAY?

HE SAYS *HALF PAY*-- AND NOT TILL MORNING. NOT TILL *MORNING.* WE'RE SCREWED WE'RE REALLY SCREWED.

SYLVIO. WE GOT NO *MONEY.* WE GOT NO *MONEY.* NO *MONEY,* NO *JUNK.*

I CAN'T MAKE IT ALL NIGHT WITHOUT A FIX. YOU *KNOW* THAT. I JUST CAN'T.

HOLD ON, HOLD ON. I'LL THINK OF SOMETHING. I'LL THINK OF SOMETHING.

RIGHT. RIGHT. GET HER NAME OUT OF THE WALLET. SPELL IT FOR ME.

THIS'LL WORK. THIS'LL WORK. I'M A GENIUS.

SOON ENOUGH.

YES. WHATEVER YOU SAY. I CAN GET MY HANDS ON SIX THOUSAND WITHIN AN HOUR. THAT'S ALL I HAVE.

YES, NO POLICE. BUT PLEASE DON'T HURT OUR LITTLE GIRL. YES, I'LL BE THERE.

OH, GLENN-- WHAT ARE WE GOING TO *DO?*

WE'RE GOING TO DO EXACTLY WHAT THEY TOLD US TO DO, DARLING.

WE'RE AT THEIR *MERCY.*

AT THE GYM.

KUKK

MEANWHILE, FRANKIE CALLS OUT JUNKIE.

IT'S *SYLVIO*, CLAY. HE'S RUNNING A *RANSOM* SCAM ON THE KID'S *PARENTS*. THAT'S RIGHT. I *ARGUED* WITH HIM BUT HE WOULDN'T *LISTEN*. AND IF THE *KINGPIN* FINDS OUT ABOUT IT *YOU* COULD GET HURT; *YOU KNOW* I DON'T WANT *YOU* GETTING HURT.

UM, CAN I COME *OVER*?... OH, *SURE*, CLAY, I'LL MEET YOU *ANYWHERE*. WE'LL HAVE A *GOOD TIME*, UM, YOU'VE GOT *MONEY*, DON'T YOU?

CLAY'S BOSS TELLS HIS BOSS.

AND HIS BOSS TELLS HIS BOSS.

AND SOMEBODY'S BOSS TELLS THE KINGPIN.

UNACCEPTABLE. CLAY'S *INCOMPETENCE* HAS CAUSED A *MESS*, LARKS. CLEAN IT UP.

YES, SIR.

DON'T *RESTRAIN* YOURSELF. MAKE IT AS *LOUD* AS YOU *WISH.* *EXAMPLES* MUST BE MADE. *DISCIPLINE* MUST BE MAINTAINED.

WE MUST TAKE WHAT ADVANTAGE WE CAN FROM THIS SORRY SITUATION. A FEW GOOD, OLD-FASHIONED, GANGSTER-STYLE *RUB-OUTS* ARE ALWAYS GOOD FOR... *REMINDING* OUR CONSTITUENCY.

OH, AND *LARKS...* THE GIRL IS *YOURS.*

VERY GOOD, SIR.

CLAY GRABS A WAD OF TWENTIES FROM THE SAFE AND HEADS FOR HIS SINFUL LITTLE RENDEZVOUS.

HE'LL ONLY NEED A *COUPLE* OF TWENTIES. IT NEVER TAKES MORE THAN *ONE FIX* TO GET A JUNKIE *AGREEABLE.*

CLAY LIKES JUNKIES. JUST GIVE ONE WHAT SHE *NEEDS*-- --AND YOU DON'T EVEN HAVE TO *TALK* TO HER, IF YOU DON'T WANT TO.

LIFE IS GOOD, HE THINKS. IT IS TO BE HIS *LAST* THOUGHT.

THREE MORE REMAIN.

FIRST THE TWO JUNKIES DIE.

THEN LARKS WILL DECIDE THE FATE OF THE GIRL.

AT HIS LEISURE.

EAST EIGHTH STREET.

MICKEY'S DAD IS *PANTING* -- MORE FROM *FEAR* THAN FROM *FATIGUE*.

RING RING

HELLO? -- YES. YES, I UNDER-STAND. WHATEVER YOU SAY. YES. I KNOW THE CORNER. YES. I'M ON MY WAY.

WHOEVER KIDNAPPED MICKEY IS *BOUNCING* THE POOR MAN ALL OVER *TOWN*, LOOKING TO SHAKE OFF ANY *COPS* WHO MIGHT BE *TAILING* HIM.

THE COPS WILL BE THE *LEAST* OF THEIR WORRIES.

@phone @phone

WEST SEVENTY-SECOND STREET.

RING RING

YES. YES. I'M ON MY WAY.

THEY RUN THE POOR MAN RAGGED.

HOK

AND THEY TEST MATT'S *PATIENCE* FOR ALL IT'S WORTH.

@phone @phon

FINALLY, IN THE SOUTH BRONX.

THE DROP-OFF.

EVERY DOLLAR HE HAS AND HE GIVES IT UP EAGERLY.

AND, HOPING AGAINST HOPE, MICKEY'S DAD DASHES OFF TOWARD A PARKING LOT WHERE THE VOICE ON THE PHONE TOLD HIM HIS GIRL WILL BE.

BUT A STREET KID FROM HELL'S KITCHEN NAMED MATT MURDOCK KNOWS BETTER THAN TO TRUST A KIDNAPPER ONCE HE'S BEEN PAID.

SO HE WAITS...

...UNTIL, FROM HIDING -- A MASS OF COLD SHAKES AND SHALLOW, TOO-FAST BREATHING.

MUTTERING TO HIMSELF.

WORKED. IT WORKED. I'M A GENIUS.

HE GRABS THE MONEY. KISSES IT. CACKLES.

BE SILENT, MATT TELLS HIMSELF. BE SNEAKY.

BE VERY, VERY SNEAKY.

A QUICK TRIP BACK INTO TOWN.

WAIT TILL SHE SEES THIS. DAMN. WAIT TILL SHE SEES THIS.

A GENIUS. I'M A GENIUS. WAIT TILL SHE SEES THIS.

THE KINGPIN WILL NEVER KNOW. THERE'S NO WAY HE'LL EVER KNOW. I'M A GENIUS.

F U P P

THE TASTE IS SALTY AND UNMISTAKABLE.

MATT GAGS-- BREAKING HIS SILENCE--

--REVEALING HIMSELF.

FUPP
FUPP FUPP
SPAK

SOON,
OUTSIDE.

NOTHING,
SIR, NOT A
SOUND. NO
SIGN OF
HIM.

YES, SIR. CLAY AND
THE JUNKIES ARE
DEAD -- AND I HAVE
THE GIRL. BUT THIS
NEW MAN -- HE MAY
BE A COP.

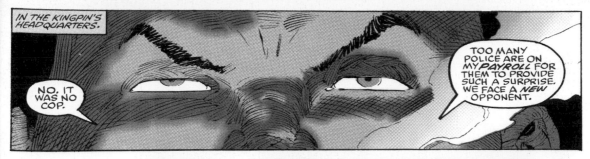

IN THE KINGPIN'S HEADQUARTERS.

NO. IT WAS NO COP.

TOO MANY POLICE ARE ON MY *PAYROLL* FOR THEM TO PROVIDE SUCH A SURPRISE. WE FACE A *NEW* OPPONENT.

PERHAPS A *VIGILANTE*-- MORE LIKELY A RIVAL *GANG.* TAKE THE GIRL TO THE MAIN DISTRIBUTION CENTER AND AWAIT INSTRUCTIONS.

YES, SIR.

MR. *SLAUGHTER*, READY YOUR *MEN.* ALL OF THEM.

YES, SIR.

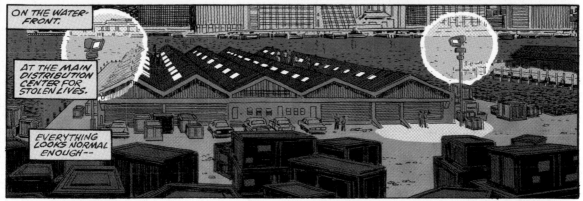

ON THE WATERFRONT.

AT THE MAIN DISTRIBUTION CENTER FOR STOLEN LIVES.

EVERYTHING LOOKS NORMAL ENOUGH--

--BUT THERE'S NASTY BUSINESS GOING ON INSIDE.

STOP IT--LET GO OF ME!

SCREAM ALL YOU WANT, KID. NOBODY CAN HEAR YOU.

NOBODY CAN HEAR.

NOBODY CAN HELP.

NOBODY CAN HEAR.

EXCEPT MAYBE ONE GUY...

AND MICKEY IS *RIGHT.*

MATT HAS TRAILED LARKS TO THIS PLACE.

...ONE GUY WHO MIGHT HAVE COME AFTER HER. ONE GUY WITH THE *BEST EARS* IN THE WHOLE *WORLD.*

HE *SCANS,* STRAINING, UNTIL...

...HE HEARS SOMETHING *FAINT.* BIRD-LIKE...

...IS THAT *SINGING?*

YES.

STRONGER NOW.

AND OTHER VOICES. ALL KIDS.

A CHORUS.

DOZENS OF CHILDREN--NOW HUNDREDS!

WHAT HAS MATT STUMBLED ONTO?

WHAT'S GOTTEN INTO *THEM?*

THIS IS GETTING PRETTY WEIRD.

JUST BUILDING THEIR *COURAGE.* THEY'LL *NEED* IT.

NICE TOUCH, JULIO. THE SINGING, I MEAN.

UM... YEAH. RIGHT. CAME UP WITH THE IDEA MYSELF. THOUGHT YOU'D LIKE IT.

OUTSIDE.

POWER CRACKLES BENEATH MATT'S FEET.

WAVES LICK ROTTING PILINGS.

THE HEART OF THE CITY *ROARS*, DISTANT, BEHIND HIM.

BUT MATT IS *QUIET*...

...QUIETER THAN THE MURMURED BRAGGING OF THE TWO MEN IN HIS WAY...

SO I TOLD HER. I TOLD HER *GOOD*.

...QUIETER, EVEN THAN THEIR HEARTBEATS.

SOMETIMES YOU JUST GOT TO *LAY DOWN* THE *LAW*, YOU KNOW?

A *LAZY* GROUP, THESE GUARDS. UNFOCUSED. NOT USED TO TROUBLE.

THEY *YAWN* AND CHAT.

ONE OF THEM *EVEN* LISTENS TO MUSIC.

NO MUSIC, STICK ALWAYS SAID. NOT WHEN YOU'RE DOING ANYTHING *ELSE*.

LISTEN TO *MUSIC* AND THERE'S NO TELLING WHAT YOU'LL MISS.

POP

KUNK!

A FEW WIRES YANKED--

--AND THERE WILL BE NO ESCAPE FOR ANY OF THEM. NOT BY CAR, ANYWAY.

TWO MORE, ON THE DOCK.

ALL THE REST ARE INSIDE.

MAKE NO SOUND.

CONCENTRATE.

DID YOU *HEAR* SOMETHING, MICK?

WHUFF

'K*REE*

THIS ONE'S *STRONG*--

--THE *OTHER* IS *FAT*--

--HIS LUNGS FILL WITH *WATER*--

--HIS *HEART DIES*--

A KNIFE-- NO CHOICE--

--GIVE IT BACK TO HIM--

--NOW--THE FAT ONE--

--HE DOESN'T FLOAT TO THE SURFACE--

--HE'S WEIGHTED DOWN--

--BY EXPLOSIVES. GRENADES.

MATT TIES THEM TO THE DOCK--

--YANKS A PIN--

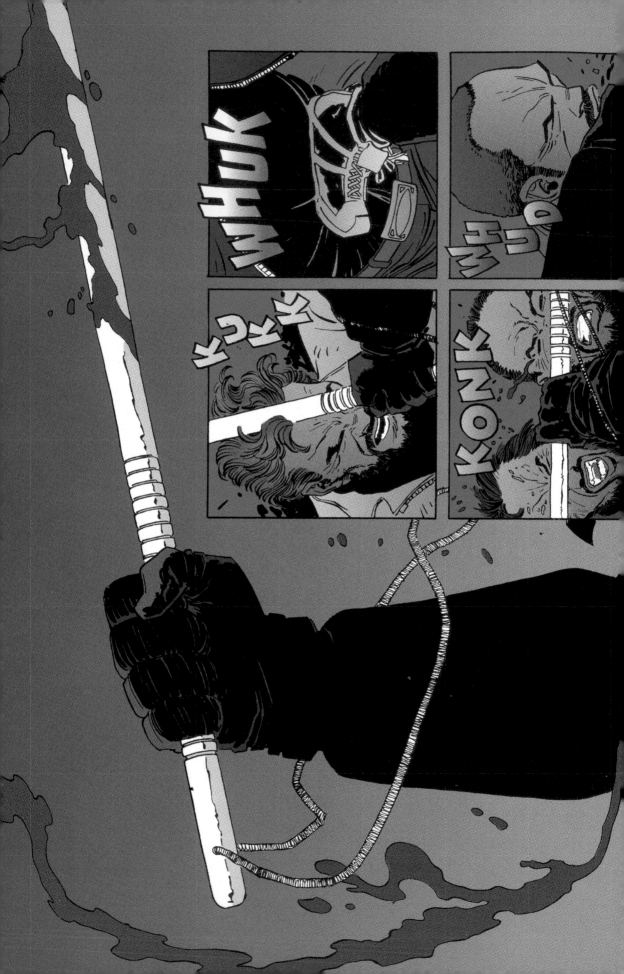

AND THE WHIRLWIND STOPS.

THERE'S NOBODY LEFT TO HIT.

BE SURE. SCAN CAREFULLY.

ONLY THE SHALLOW BREATHING OF THE UNCONSCIOUS.

THE LOW MOANS OF THE HELPLESS.

AND...

...FROM INSIDE-- AN ENGINE ROARS TO LIFE...

CRASH!

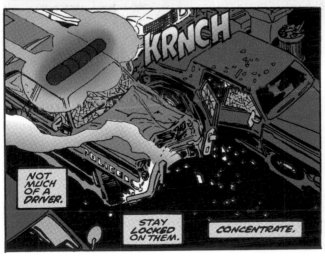

STAY LOCKED. STAY LOCKED.

THERE. NOW.

CRASHH

A DEAD MOMENT-- FIGHT IT--

--LET THE RAIN DE-SCRIBE THEM--

--CATCH THEIR SCENT--

--STAY LOCKED--

--FOLLOW THEM--AS BEST YOU CAN...

KRAK

SILENCE NOW, SWEETHEART. EVERYTHING'S GOING TO BE FINE...

LET...

HNH?

THE NAME FLITS THROUGH THE KING-PIN'S MIND, ANNOY-ING, PERSISTENT.

ONE MAN HAS SHAT-TERED AN OPERATION THAT WAS THE WORK OF YEARS. ONE MAN HAS COST HIM MIL-LIONS. ONE MAN HAS COST HIM DOZENS OF HIS LIEUTENANTS, ALL TOSSED AS SCAPEGOATS TO THE POLICE IN THE WAKE OF THE LARGEST BUST IN THE CITY'S HISTORY.

BUT SOON THE COPS WILL HAVE THEIR HEADLINES AND EVERYTHING WILL BE BACK IN ORDER. THE KINGPIN WILL NOT BE TOUCHED-- AND HIS EMPIRE WILL GROW AGAIN, RAPACIOUS, AS IMMORTAL AS HUMAN SIN.

AND IT WILL NOT BE TOO VERY OFTEN THAT THIS PARTICU-LAR BULLY WONDERS...

BY THE TIME THE COPS ARRIVE, MATT IS GONE--LEAVING A MYSTERY AND THE FIRST RUMBLINGS OF A LEGEND.

DAREDEVIL.

THE NAME IS TO BE HEARD AGAIN--FROM QUIVERING THUGS AND FROM GRATE-FUL VICTIMS.

DAREDEVIL.

IT IS THE NAME OF A SHADOWED DEMON--AN UNSEEN AVENGER-- A SILENT, INVISIBLE SAVIOR OF THE INNOCENT.

DAREDEVIL.

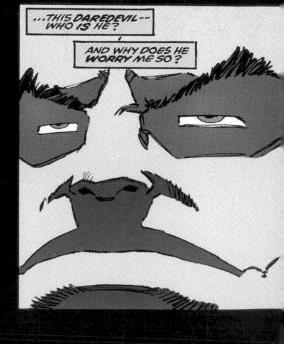

...THIS DAREDEVIL-- WHO IS HE?

AND WHY DOES HE WORRY ME SO?

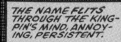

MATT MURDOCK SITS IN THE RAIN AND LAUGHS.

HIS DAY BEGAN WITH A RINGING *PHONE* AND AN ANGRY *VOICE.*

IT WAS HIS *BOSS.* FROM *BOSTON.* TELLING HIM HE'S *FIRED.*

THAT WAS WHEN MATT STARTED LAUGHING. IT MADE HIS *BOSS* SO FURIOUS HE *HUNG UP* ON MATT. BUT STILL MATT COULDN'T STOP *LAUGHING.*

BOSTON.

MATT COULDN'T LEAVE NEW YORK NOW IF HE *WANTED* TO.

THE BOY FROM HELL'S KITCHEN HAS COME *HOME.*

HOME--TO A NEW LIFE.

THEN IT'S A *DEAL,* MATT! MY *DAD* WILL LEND US THE MONEY FOR AN *OFFICE,* PROVIDED IT'S NOT TOO *FANCY.*

WE WON'T NEED ANYTHING FANCY, FOGGY. NOT FOR THE KIND OF WORK WE'VE GOT IN FRONT OF US. ALL THAT STUFF WE TALKED ABOUT IN *COLLEGE--* ALL THOSE *IDEALS--* WE CAN *DO* IT, FOGGY.

THEN WE'RE ALL *SET*--ONCE WE FIGURE OUT WHOSE NAME COMES *FIRST* ON THE *DOOR.* IS IT *MURDOCK* AND *NELSON* OR *NELSON* AND *MURDOCK?*

I SAY WE *FLIP.* A *COIN,* I MEAN.

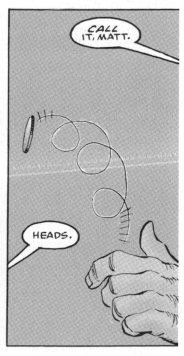

CALL IT, MATT.

HEADS.

OOPS!-- OH, GOLLY...

DOWN THE COUNTER--

FPP

--A FAMILIAR SCENT.

A PRESENCE LONG MISSED-- AND NEVER FORGOTTEN.

STICK.

STICK TAKES HIS TIME FINISHING HIS COFFEE.

EVEN AS MATT'S HEART TRIES TO CLIMB UP MATT'S THROAT.

WATCH YOUR BACK, KID.

AND THE QUARTER, IT CAME UP TAILS--

--SO YOU COME IN SECOND--

--SO DON'T YOU GET COCKY.

Daredevil: The Man Without Fear #2 Cover (1993) Artwork by John Romita Jr. & Al Williamson

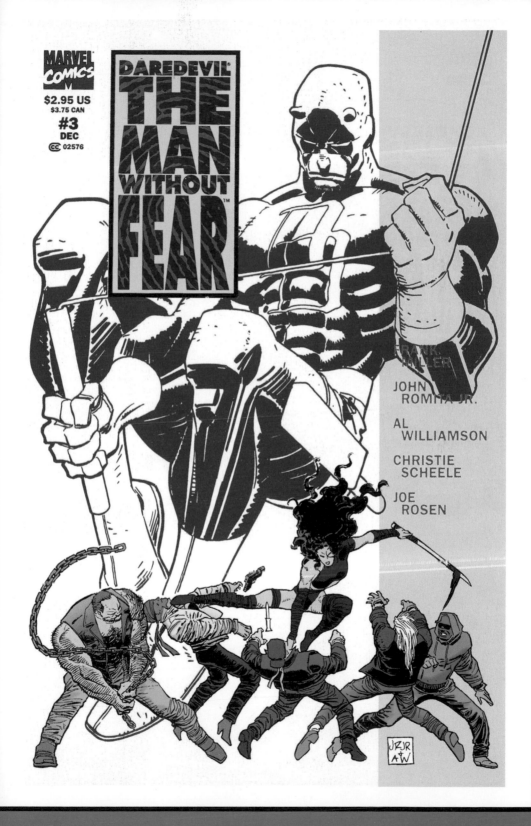

Daredevil: The Man Without Fear #3 Cover (1993) Artwork by John Romita Jr. & Al Williamson

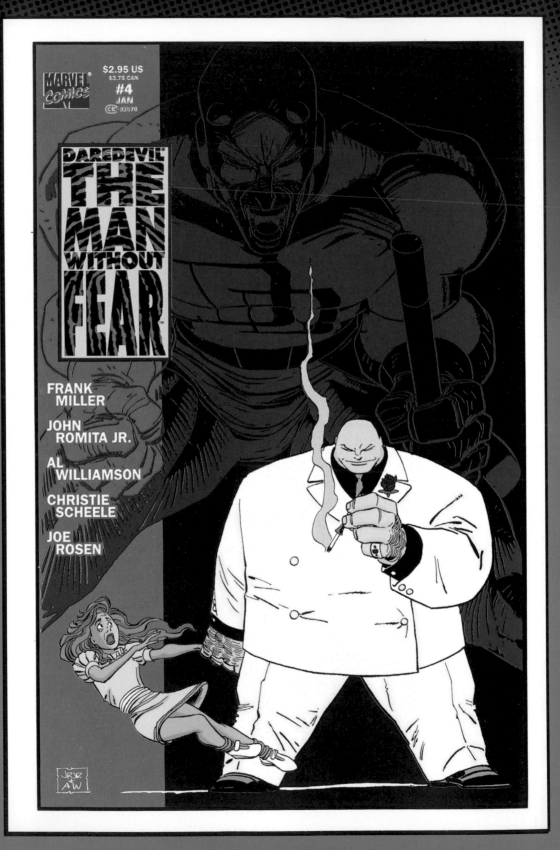

Daredevil: The Man Without Fear #4 Cover (1994) Artwork by John Romita Jr. & Al Williamson

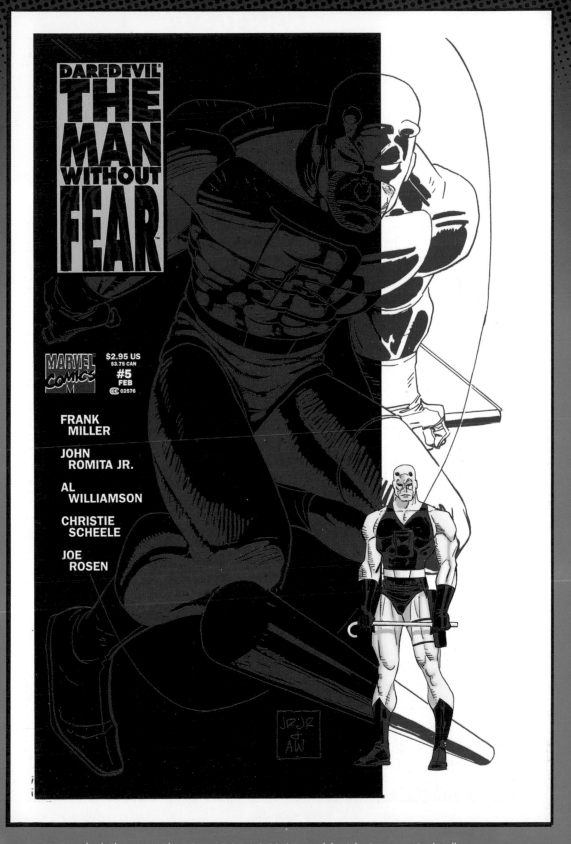

Daredevil: The Man Without Fear #5 Cover (1994) Artwork by John Romita Jr. & Al Williamson

BEHIND THE SCENES

DAREDEVIL

WHEN STAN LEE DESCRIBED HIS NEWEST CREATION AS "DIFFERENT FROM ALL OTHER SUPER-HEROES" ON THE COVER OF DAREDEVIL #1, HE WASN'T KIDDING! READ ON TO DISCOVER THE ORIGINS OF THIS INCREDIBLE TRAIL-BLAZING HERO!

STAN WITHOUT FEAR

It took **Marvel** a few tries to really get going with **Daredevil**. In the character's first year or so of publication he went through a number of main artists, and changed costumes surprisingly early on – even by super-hero standards. Once he did settle in, however, Daredevil became one of the company's most consistently compelling heroes. Since the 1980s a succession of glittering creators, from comics icon **Frank Miller** and film director **Kevin Smith** to Marvel stalwarts **Brian Michael Bendis** and **Mark Waid**, have had some of their most critically acclaimed and commercially successful work focus on the character.

Daredevil was created by **Stan Lee** in conjunction with artist **Bill Everett**, who had originally created the 1930s character **Namor the Sub-Mariner**, later repurposed by Marvel. "I wanted something for Bill to do," Lee would later recount. "He was one of the great talents in our business, and as far as I knew he wasn't doing anything – so I had to dream something up for him!" That something turned out to be blind lawyer **Matt Murdock** – better known as the vigilante Daredevil, a name previously used by a 1940s super-hero, but which had fallen out of use.

"A number of people had written articles in different papers and magazines about the fact that all of the heroes that I had come up with were flawed," Stan shares. "So, I thought, well, I had to find another guy with a flaw, because that's what turned people on to our books!"

Recalling something he'd read about the heightened senses present in some cases of blindness, Lee decided to apply this in the extreme to a super-powered character.

RED DEVIL

Everett was ultimately only able to draw the first issue, in April 1964, before struggling to meet deadlines, and so **Joe Orlando** filled in for the next issues before the much-trumpeted arrival of **Wally Wood**, the legendary *Mad* writer/artist. Wood's first order of business on *Daredevil* was to design a new costume – the original yellow number, which had been created by Everett with input from **Jack Kirby**, was disliked by readers, so Lee instructed Wood to come up with an entirely red outfit instead. Unfortunately while Wood's run – in which he also co-plotted stories – was well received, it was also brief, as he left the book after issue #11.

The next artist through the door was **John Romita Sr.**, a penciller who had expressed a desire to move solely to inking but was lured back to draw *Daredevil* from issue #12, to help Lee out in an emergency. Staying on for a little over six months revitalised Romita's artistic career, and saw him move over to *Amazing Spider-Man* in 1966 – but once again, it left the nascent Daredevil series in dire need of a regular artist.

THE COLAN COMETH

Fortunately, the next penciller to take on the task would stick around significantly longer, and indeed become one of Daredevil's quintessential artists: **Gene Colan**, who stayed with the book from issue #20 in September 1966 all the way through to issue #100 in June 1973. Colan's handle on the character was so masterful that Lee also trusted him to play a more active role in plotting Daredevil's adventures. While Colan's run as an artist was lengthy, throughout the 1970s it was the writers who began to

change on a regular basis. **Roy Thomas**, **Gerry Conway** and **Steve Gerber** all had notable, brief stints, but following the tenures of **Marv Wolfman** and **Jim Shooter**, by the end of the decade the character's sales and popularity had waned. It was the arrival of a young artist named **Frank Miller** that would rapidly change Daredevil's fortunes.

MILLER'S MURDOCK

"I got to draw a couple of issues of the secondary *Spider-Man* title," explains Miller, "and they guest-starred this character Daredevil that I'd never really paid attention to. But I kind of dug him, because... Well, how many super-heroes are known for what they *can't* do? I thought this guy could be the perfect hard-boiled superhero!"

He began drawing *Daredevil* with issue #158 in May 1979 – and by issue #168, Miller persuaded Marvel to let him take over as sole writer from the outgoing **Roger McKenzie**. This began a seminal two-year run in which the writer/artist revitalised the character with a dark, powerful and gritty take – and as much as this was controversial (Miller describing the reaction as being, "as if I'd brought whisky into a playground"), it was also hugely popular. Two further stints by him as writer would follow – first with **David Mazzucchelli** for the seminal *Born Again* storyline in 1985, and later with **John Romita Jr.** on the undisputed classic, *The Man Without Fear* in 1993.

Miller's run established Murdock as one of Marvel's most consistently popular characters, which he remains to this day – and the iconic writer/artist is in no doubt as to why he appeals to readers and creators alike. "Daredevil is the guy I punish for all my mistakes and sins," Miller explains, "because he really is a flawed hero, in that he's a man who intends to do good, and causes much damage.

"Daredevil should have been a villain," he grins, "but somehow he redeems himself and moves ahead. He just doesn't give up."

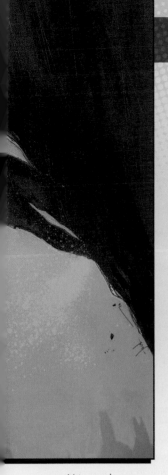

AT A YOUNG AGE, MATT MURDOCK HAD HIS VISION TAKEN FROM HIM – JUST BECAUSE HE TRIED TO DO THE RIGHT THING. THOUGH HIS LIFE HAS BEEN DEFINED BY TRAGEDY, HE HAS ALWAYS STRIVED TO KEEP TO HIS HEROIC PRINCIPLES. NOW DISCOVER THE INCREDIBLE HISTORY OF THE MAN WITHOUT FEAR!

BATTLING JACK

Matthew Michael Murdock grew up the son of **Jonathan "Battling Jack" Murdock**, a professional boxer from Hell's Kitchen, New York, who had fallen on hard times. Matt's mother, **Maggie**, left them when he was a young boy, though Jack foolishly told him that she had died to spare the boy any more pain. As Jack got older, he had to take work from a number of petty criminals to make ends meet, and when the **Fixer** threatened his son, Jack was forced into becoming an enforcer for the villain.

While Matt was a natural athlete and prankster, Jack sought to prevent him from entering his world of violence, instead hoping that Matt could gain an education that would take him away from the mean streets of Hell's Kitchen. Jack made his son swear that he would study hard and never use his fists – Matt, however, was brutally bullied at school, callously referred to as "Daredevil", and when he lashed out at the other children in retaliation, Jack struck him. Matt began to understand the importance of rules and laws, and the evil they prohibit – it was during this time that he decided to become a lawyer. Struggling under the increased pressure from his father and his studies, Matt worked out his frustrations at the local gym, observed from the shadows by a mysterious man known only as **"Stick"**.

EXTRASENSORY

Matt's life was changed forever the day he witnessed an out-of-control truck speeding toward an elderly man struggling to crossing the road. Matt pushed him to safety, avoiding the truck, but a container housing strange chemicals hit the ground and spilled into his eyes. He awoke days later to discover that the chemicals had left him blind. His other senses, however, were inexplicably strengthened – to an excruciating degree. The boy's pain was soothed by a visiting nun, **Sister Maggie** – unbeknown to him, she was his mother, who had left her family to join a nearby convent in New York. Sister Maggie told Matt that although his powers were a blessing, he must keep them secret. As he struggled to adapt to this new way of life, Matt attempted to resume his training, but found that moves he had previously mastered now seemed impossible. It was at this time that Stick, a blind martial-arts master, came to him.

Under his new sensei's harsh guidance, Matt came to understand his newly developed senses and blossomed into a formidable fighter. Soon after, Battling Jack

MATT MURDOCK'S MOST ICONIC ISSUES

Daredevil #1 (1963)

The Man Without Fear makes his daring debut in Daredevil #1!

Daredevil #7 (1965)

Matt's iconic red costume makes its first appearance

Daredevil #158 (1979)

Frank Miller takes over as the primary scribe on the series

refused to throw a boxing match and was brutally murdered by the Fixer's hired muscle. Although explicitly instructed not to go after them by Stick, Matt chased his father's killers down and viciously attacked them. He struggled with the last criminal in a brothel hideout, and inadvertently caused a prostitute to fall to her death, as the last of his father's killers escaped scot-free. Dismayed by the outcome, Matt ran back to the gym to find Stick – only to discover that, for the first time in his life, he was truly alone.

NELSON & MURDOCK

Matt continued to study, and eventually attended Columbia State University, majoring in pre-Law. He met **Franklin "Foggy" Nelson**, who quickly became his closest friend. Soon after, Matt met **Elektra Natchios**, a strikingly beautiful woman with whom he was quickly smitten. Though she initially dismissed him, Matt showed off his acrobatic prowess, and found in Elektra a kindred spirit. They quickly fell in love and, for a while, their romance was euphoric. Elektra soon fled the country, however, when her father, a rich businessman with ties to the mob, was taken hostage and murdered. Once again, Matt was left alone, heartbroken. When his

friend Mickey was abducted by the Kingpin of Crime, **Wilson Fisk**'s men, the young man, dressed all in black, successfully abolished Fisk's child-trafficking empire. As rumours of this vigilante "Daredevil" began to swirl within the underworld, Matt fashioned himself a striking costume, inspired by the duality of faith that had hung so heavily over his mother. In that moment, a hero was born.

Keen for a fresh start, and to administer justice on both sides of the law, Matt transferred to Harvard Law School, with Foggy not far behind. Upon graduating, the two moved to New York City, where Matt was confident he could make a difference to the citizens of Hell's Kitchen. He joined Foggy, establishing the **Nelson & Murdock** law firm (Matt took second billing after losing a coin toss), on 58th Street in New York City. Foggy hired a beautiful young woman, **Karen Page**, to work as the pair's secretary; both he and Matt were soon infatuated.

Professionally, Matt was soon appointed to be a lawyer for the **Fantastic Four**, a family of super-heroes empowered by cosmic rays. The quartet's presence, like Matt's incredible powers, signalled a significant change in New York – more and more heroes began to appear across the city, and indeed, America. As a crimefighter, Matt's life was also becoming more complicated – in the following months, he fought against super-powered villains **Electro**, the **Owl**, the **Purple Man** and **Stilt-Man**. In the time since Karen had joined the firm, she and Matt

An electrifying comicbook icon makes her debut in Daredevil #168!

Frank Miller and David Mazzucchelli present the industry-defining *Born Again*

Miller teams up with John Romita Jr. to present the definitive Daredevil origin

Matt struggles with his faith as Foggy discovers the truth of his hidden identity

had fallen deeply in love, although frustrations arose as his vigilantism got in the way of their relationship. In a subsequent struggle with the salacious **"Starr" Saxon**, the criminal learned Dardevil's true identity, which was also uncovered by T'Challa, the Wakandan hero known to the world as the **Black Panther**. Hoping to eliminate any potential threats to Karen and his friends, Matt faked his own death in an aeroplane explosion. After the apparent death of Saxon (by this time the masked menace, **Mister Fear**), Matt returned to the grieving Karen and revealed his true identity to her. He proposed to her, and she accepted – but only if he gave up his double life as the horned hero. Matt confessed that he couldn't stand by as innocents were threatened, and Karen left him, moving to Los Angeles to pursue an acting career.

BLACK WIDOW

When a mysterious villain, **Mr Kline**, ordered the Owl to kill Daredevil, he was saved by Natasha Romanoff, the super-spy **Black Widow**, leading to an alliance between the two. Together, they moved to San Francisco; when a news reporter drew attention to the fact that esteemed lawyer Matthew Murdock and the costumed vigilante Daredevil had simultaneously arrived in the city, Matt had the Black Panther impersonate him on the streets of New York, successfully eliminating the suspicion of Murdock being the masked super-hero. When Matt's senior partner, the esteemed **Kerwin J. Broderick**, transformed himself into the monstrous Earth-creature **Terrex**, Daredevil and his allies were forced to destroy Terrex, killing Broderick in the process. Feeling his work in New York was not yet done, Matt headed home soon

after. When reporter **Ben Urich** discovered Matt's secret identity, he tried to deny it, but finally conceded to Urich, beginning a close relationship between the two that would last for years. Matt soon learned that Elektra was in fact

alive, and had trained to become an assassin, attempting to break free from her father's grasp. When **Bullseye** was hired by a unknown benefactor to take down the Kingpin he went after Fisk – only to be offered a substantially larger sum by his target if he worked for him exclusively. Returning from incarceration at the hands of Daredevil, Bullseye was furious to discover that Fisk had hired Elektra as his replacement. Out of spite for the two of them, Bullseye murdered Elektra. Matt beat the villain within an inch of his life, crippling him.

Matt briefly regained his sight via the virtually omnipotent alien, the **Beyonder**, after which he and the arachnid hero Spider-Man revealed their secret identities to each other during a struggle against the crazed **Sin-Eater**, markedly strengthening their friendship. In what would become one of Matt's darkest periods, the hero soon discovered that Karen Page had become an addict, and had sold his identity in exchange for drugs. This information made its way to the Kingpin, who used it to tear his enemy's life apart – Matt's law license was revoked, his bank accounts were frozen, and his apartment was blown up. Matt attacked Fisk, who very nearly killed him in retaliation. Narrowly escaping the crimelord, the semiconscious Matt was discovered by Sister Maggie, who nursed him back to health.

BORN AGAIN

Eventually recovering, Matt made his peace with the rehabilitated Karen, and he started a free legal clinic. When his work thwarted the illegal operations of the Kingpin, Fisk sent the criminally insane, psionic super-villain **Typhoid Mary** to destroy Matt, once and for all. She nearly succeeded, but left the hero severely disillusioned by his secret life. After a brief sabbatical, he was able to commit Mary to a mental asylum, and

Daredevil Vol. 2 #1 (1998)

Daredevil Vol. 2 #16 (2001)

Daredevil: Yellow #1 (2001)

Ultimate Marvel Team-Up #1 (2001)

Director Kevin Smith and Marvel Knights maestro Joe Quesada reinvent Daredevil

Brian Michael Bendis begins his gritty, legendary run on *Daredevil Vol. 2!*

The first of comics dream team Jeph Loeb and Tim Sale's Marvel 'Colour' series

The Daredevil makes his Ultimate debut, fighting alongside Spider-Man and the Punisher

topple the Kingpin from power. This happiness would be short-lived however, as the reporter **Sara Harrington** ransacked Ben Urich's files, and exposed Matt's identity in a tabloid newspaper.

Desperate, Matt was forced to take the identity of **Jack Batlin**, in homage to his father, and adopt a new, darker, more durable grey Daredevil costume. After overcoming his inner demons, he rediscovered his purpose in life, and emerged from his self-imposed exile. The tabloid accusations having been discredited, Matt joined **Rosalind Sharpe**, Foggy's mother, at her new law firm. Soon after, the special effects specialist super-criminal **Mysterio**, learning that he was dying of cancer, wanted to go out with a bang. Discovering Matt's secret identity, he set about wrecking the hero's life – framing Foggy for murder, straining Matt's Catholic faith to breaking point, and having Bullseye callously murder Karen, as she protected a baby integral to Mysterio's twisted plot. The villain eventually ended his own life, and Matt, mourning the greatest love of his life, used Karen's inheritance to re-establish Nelson & Murdock in the grounds of his old apartment block.

EXPOSED

The up-and-coming criminal **Sammy Silke** soon arranged an ambush on the Kingpin that left the crimelord half-dead. Silke escaped death at the hands of Fisk's wife **Vanessa**, surrendering information to the FBI – including

Dardevil's secret identity. Agent **Henry Dobbs** sold Daredevil's identity to the *Daily Globe* newspaper, which printed it as a front page story. Matt publicly and vehemently denied he was Daredevil, even going so far as to sue the *Globe's* president for libel

– though the *Globe* was forced to renounce their stance on the matter, the public at large remained sceptical of Matt's disconnection from his alter-ego. Matt began dating **Milla Donvan**, and the two secretly became an item after just a short period together. Frustrated by the corruption in New York, Matt launched an all-out retaliation against the Kingpin, with the aid of his super-heroic "bodyguard" allies, **Jessica Jones** and **Luke Cage**.

WITHOUT FEAR

He ably defeated a recently released Typhoid Mary, and stopped Bullseye from making Milla the third love of his to meet death at his hands. Publicly defeating Fisk, Matt took over the role of the Kingpin. Following Milla's announcement that she was leaving him, due to a number of revelations on the part of Ben Urich, Matt sank into darkness. Taking control of the mystical ninja clan the **Hand**, he erected a fortress in the heart of Hell's Kitchen, over the area where Bullseye had blown up a residential block, dubbed the Shadowland. Earth's Mightiest Heroes rushed to save Matt's soul as he became further corrupted by a mystical entity known as the **Beast**, but not before he brutally murdered Bullseye. Spider-Man, Luke Cage and their street-level allies were eventually victorious, but Matt emerged a shadow of his former self.

What followed was a journey of rebirth for the hero, as he travelled across New Mexico. Foiling the plot of a corrupt police force, he realised that there *was* in fact a place for Daredevil in the world, and he returned to New York to rebuild both aspects of his life. Since then, Matt has enjoyed a new lease of life, embracing the joys of his role as Daredevil, and integrating himself into the wider Marvel Universe. Operating as one of New York's premier heroes, the Man Without Fear truly is one of Marvel's Mightiest Heroes.

Shadowland #1 (2010)

Daredevil Vol. 3 #1 (2011)

Daredevil: End of Days #1 (2012)

Daredevil Vol. 4 #1 (2014)

Daredevil's descent into darkness comes full circle as he battles Bullseye to the death

Following Matt's resurrection in *Daredevil: Reborn*, Mark Waid and Paolo Rivera reset the status quo

Brian Michael Bendis' last testament, *End of Days* is a fitting epilogue

The Man Without Fear relocates to San Francisco to build a new crime-fighting life!

FURTHER READING

I F YOU'VE ENJOYED THE UNCANNY ORIGINS OF DAREDEVIL AND WOULD LIKE TO DISCOVER MORE LEGENDS OF THE MAN WITHOUT FEAR, HERE ARE SOME OTHER MARVEL GRAPHIC NOVELS WE RECOMMEND...

**Daredevil
Born Again**

At the book shop:
ISBN: 9780785134817

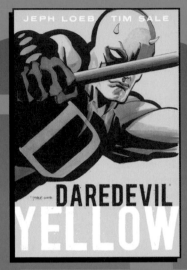

**Daredevil
Yellow**

At the book shop:
ISBN: 9780785109693

**Daredevil
By Bendis & Maleev
Ultimate Collection**

At the book shop:
ISBN: 9780785143888

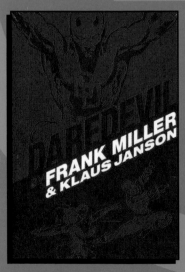

**Daredevil By Frank Miller
and Klaus Janson Omnibus**

At the book shop:
ISBN: 9780785185680

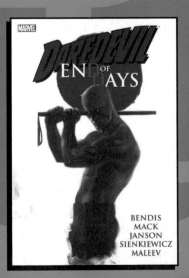

**Daredevil
End of Days**

At the book shop:
ISBN: 9780785124207

**Daredevil
Devil at Bay**

At the book shop:
ISBN: 9780785154112